CHRISTIAN EXCELLENCE

ALTERNATIVE TO SUCCESS

CHRISTIAN EXCELLENCE

ALTERNATIVE TO SUCCESS

Jon Johnston

Nazarene Publishing House
Kansas City, Missouri

First printing, May 1985
Second printing, January 1986
Third printing, July 1986

Printed in the United States of America

Unless otherwise indicated, all Scripture references are from the Holy Bible: New International Version, copyright © 1973, 1978 by the International Bible Society.

The author wishes to express his appreciation for permission to reprint "Success" by David Neff, by permission of *His*, student magazine of Inter-Varsity Christian Fellowship, © 1984; the Temperament Test, taken from *After Every Wedding Comes a Marriage Workbook*, copyright 1981, Harvest House Publishers, 1075 Arrowsmith, Eugene, Oregon 97402; the Trenton Spiritual Gifts Analysis, copyright Fuller Evangelistic Association, Box 989, Pasadena, California 91102, no further reprint authorization is granted; and "I Wonder" by Ruth Harms Calkin, from *Tell Me Again, Lord, I Forget*, published by Tyndale House Publishing, Inc., © 1974 by Ruth Harms Calkin, used by permission.

To my beautiful wife,
Cherry,
whose constant encouragement,
helpful editing,
and consistent life
of Christian excellence
made this book possible.

Success is the key they hand you when they like you.
It doesn't matter why.
They just give you the key that unlocks an upscale condo,
triggers the powerful purr of your new Mercedes,
and accesses the executive washroom.
It's what they give to you.

Excellence is another brand of brazil nut.
It's what's within you.
It's what you do
that stretches mind and muscle.

They'll hand you success when your ratings are up,
your sales soar, or when the eager masses
plunk down their grubby bucks to buy your stuff.
And they'll snatch success away at daybreak.

Success loves its one-night stands at the Ritz.
But never expect it to say, I do.
Success is a day-tripper and a tease.
Success'll forget you.

Excellence endures when the crowd moves on.

David Neff

Contents

Foreword   **11**
Preface   **15**

Part **1** **Excellence:** *Need of the World*

1   Enough Is Enough!   **21**

2   Competing Ideals: *Excellence and Success*   **29**

3   The Greeks Had a Word for It   **35**

Part **2** **Excellence:** *Norm of God's Word*

4   Understanding with Open Mind   **45**

5   Pursuing with Fervent Heart   **61**

Part **3** **Excellence:** *Nurtured in Our Walk*

6   The Towel and the Cross   **77**

7   Lowly, But Not Losers   **91**

8   The Joy of Unmasking   **105**

9   Webs of Love   **121**

10 Refusing to Cry "Uncle"   **137**

11 We Are All Gifted   **151**

12 Daring to Act   **167**

A Parting Word   **185**

Appendixes

A   Trenton Spiritual Gifts Analysis   **189**

B   Temperament Test   **207**

Subject Index   **215**

Scripture Index   **224**

Foreword

Two dangers threaten the survival of Christendom. The one is mediocrity; the other is success. We have been tempted by both of them. Jon Johnston, in his book, provides an alternative to either of them. That alternative is excellence.

Mediocrity has come to characterize the behavior of most people in most of our institutions. People grow up in homes with mediocre parents, receive a mediocre education, become mediocre in their productivity in industries that reek of mediocrity. They live out their Christian commitment in a mediocre fashion within the context of churches that have mediocre programs. It is not surprising that Jon Johnston, speaking as one committed to the Holiness tradition of Christianity, should find mediocrity to be intolerable. He refuses to allow the admonition of Christ to be "perfect" to be viewed as an unattainable goal that no one is expected to achieve, although nice to have for motivational purposes. Johnston makes it clear that excellence is a requirement of the Christian. To him, holiness is excellence. Love is excellence and being Christian is excellence.

In a Christian world, in which there has been an oversell of "cheap grace," Johnston reminds us that followers of Christ must "work out their own salvation" by developing the lifestyle that results in the maximum employment of one's gifts and service for others. He makes us see that godliness is a lifestyle in which a person is called to become all he or she could be in Christ.

Although Johnston is familiar with the best-selling book by Thomas J. Peters and Robert H. Waterman, Jr., *In Search of Excellence,* it should not be assumed that he follows their value system. Those who have read the work of Peters and Waterman know that they view excellence as a means to achieve success. So far as Johnston is concerned, success, as this world understands it, is not the goal of the Christian. Wealth, power, and prestige, the common marks and symbols of worldly success, are not things that Christians are to aspire to possess. Instead, says Johnston, we are called to a simple lifestyle in which wealth is utilized to bless the less fortunate. Power is abandoned in the adopting of a lifestyle of servanthood and prestige is discarded in favor of Christian humility. While rejecting the values of this world, Johnston makes it clear that we are still called to excellence. We are called to be efficient, committed, creative, and productive. However, all of these dimensions of personality are viewed in a different way as Johnston reinterprets them from biblical perspectives.

Evangelicalism has undergone fantastic growth in the past five years. Its numerical expansion and its heightened prestige have been conducive to the development of a "success theology." Those who propagate this new belief system argue that those who follow the teachings of Scripture and imitate Jesus will become a success in any ventures they enter. To become followers of Jesus means for the propagators of the success theology that Christians will be champions in athletics, winners in races for political office, victorious in beauty contests, and leaders in business. They argue that the Christian lifestyle is a guaranteed route to the financial rewards that belong to the elite. Trusting in God will make all kinds of good things happen, from helping us to find parking places on crowded city streets to winning Olympic medals. Many contemporary revivalist meetings have the characteristics of Amway conventions. This is not surprising, since the principles of Scripture have been transformed into the criteria of success prescribed for Amway salespersons. All in all, Christianity has become a theodicy of good fortune for all too many in this second half of the twentieth century.

Over and against the success theology stands the work of Johnston. He helps us to remember that the followers of Jesus did not end up with expensive houses, money in the bank, and social prestige. He reminds us that the apostles, who, more than any since their day, have lived out the principles of God's Word in their imitation of their Master, ended up despised, rejected, impoverished, beaten, and eventually crucified. He reminds us that the excellence that is required of Christians in their everyday walk has no nexus with the success symbols which have increasingly become the symbols of "good" Christians.

Servanthood, powerlessness, and sacrifice are not prominent concepts in the mind-set of contemporary evangelicals. They know the words, but they do not know how to set them to music and hence they do not know how to play them out in the world. Johnston makes these traits core to the Christian lifestyle. He provides concrete direction for all who have chosen to follow Christ, our excellent example. The book is a call to servantlike, simple, sincere, inclusive, uncompromising, stewardly, and assertive excellence. It is a call to act with power and conviction. It is a challenge to change the world for Christ via the embracing of a value system of behavioral principles that many might consider countercultural.

Holiness is excellence, so there is no excuse for mediocrity. Success is worldly, so there is no excuse for Christians pursuing it. These are things that we must learn. These are things that Johnston teaches us effectively. In the words of the apostle Paul, we must "press on toward the goal to win the prize for which God has called [us] heavenward in Christ Jesus" (Phil. 3:14). To all who would pursue this, the rest of the book will prove worthy.

Anthony Campolo, Jr.

Preface

Like so many people, I once associated excellence with flawlessness. The excellent person never makes mistakes, is always consistent and confident, and is continuously applauded by scores of imperfect, jealous admirers.

My misconception produced guilt and disappointment as my shortcomings stubbornly lingered like barnacles on a pier. The gnawing thought persisted: I was destined to a life of ineptitude. As a result, I was bound to fail myself, others, and God. Before I could become fulfilled, something had to occur. Either I must drastically improve my level of performance, or I must take another look at the meaning of excellence.

It was then that I read *In Search of Excellence*, a best seller by Thomas J. Peters and Robert H. Waterman, Jr. Suddenly, excellence began to seem attainable. I came to deeply desire a more abundant earthly existence, believing that a true Christian could not do less. But my picture of excellence was cloudy and distorted. Like so many people, I failed to see the important distinction between excellence and success. In my mind the two were interchangeable.

Another book, Anthony Campolo's *Success Fantasy*, came to my attention. My distorted vision was corrected as I realized that success must not be the life-motivating goal of God's children. To make it so is to compromise biblical values and to enthrone self.

But how could I distinguish excellence and success? How could I fully comprehend, in order to achieve, an excellence that would bring glory to my heavenly Father?

I turned to God's Word, where excellence is mentioned often. My study provided inspiration and helpful direction. The temptation was to stop here. After all, my curiosity had been satisfied. My questions had been answered. I grasped a biblical ideal that would last through eternity.

However, a penetrating thought came to mind: Perhaps others have likewise sought and found sustenance by exploring this concept. Perhaps they have perceptions they would be willing to share. The thought prompted action.

I contacted *Eternity*, which graciously loaned me its mailing list of the most noteworthy scholars and leaders of the evangelical world. To these gifted and dedicated Christians I sent a survey that contained three questions: What is Christian excellence? Why do you feel that it is so necessary today? What are the greatest barriers to attaining Christian excellence?

The response was overwhelming! College presidents, magazine editors, writers, and speakers of renown generously sent a great volume of valuable, God-inspired insights. It took weeks for me to carefully digest this information.

Now I desire to share what I have learned about Christian excellence. My book issues an invitation to journey on this less-traveled road that leads to the "crown of glory that will never fade away" (1 Peter 5:4). My fervent prayer is that its pages will offer encouragement and guidance as we reach for, and grasp, our full spiritual potential. The One whose name is called "excellent" would have it so and promises to lovingly lead us in a "more excellent way" (1 Cor. 12:31, KJV).

Part 1

Excellence
Need of the World

Excellent things are as difficult as they are rare.
—Baruch Spinoza

An excellent plumber is infinitely more admirable than an incompetent philosopher. — John W. Gardner, *Excellence: Can We Be Equal and Excellent Too?*

Don't stick with me, this is a mess-up! — Nervous bank robber

1

Enough Is Enough!

Any fiftieth wedding anniversary is a special occasion, especially when it involves your parents. And when your caring, perfectionist wife labors as hard as mine did to make the event successful, you hope that every detail will be right.

Nature did its best. It was a perfect day in Pasadena. All were in the best of spirits, especially my parents. The day was "one big smile"—almost. The florist forgot to deliver the flowers!

This was the one item that Cherry had arranged for months in advance. Everything had been neatly written out. She had made the customary triple-check and a telephone call to remind just hours before the reception.

I can shut my eyes and again visualize all those bare tables, looking as blank as a plate of lard. The frustrated look in the eyes of my beautiful hostess, who struggled to maintain her characteristic poise and charm. The desperate attempt to pick flowers growing in the churchyard.

And one sight I shall never erase from my mind. The

21

reception was over. The pictures had been taken. The awkward attempts to lessen the discomfort by making "flower jokes" had been made. In fact, everyone except the family had departed. Only we were standing there, dismantling the tables. In drove the delivery truck. Out stepped a red-faced man dressed in his golf outfit. His arms were filled with impeccable arrangements. This "picture of efficiency" quickly walked up to us and said, "So sorry. I promised my wife that I'd deliver these flowers on the way to play golf. I guess I just forgot."

What could we say? The very sight of this penitent in golf clothes, with some broken tees still poked in the side of his hat, could evoke only laughter. We forgave him and assured him that the occasion went well anyhow. We just thought we needed posies, when they were no doubt a foolish extra. He smiled and returned to his irate wife with his flowers and our request for a refund.

They're Out to Get Me

Such ineptness is repeated in my life on an almost daily basis. It began on the first day of my life, when they delivered my mother the wrong baby. She had to (no doubt reluctantly) exchange that petite, beautiful female infant for me. It has been downhill ever since!

People constantly misspell my name. What's so confusing about the name *Jon Johnston?* Once I received an award. The first words were "Presented to John Jonston." Perhaps I expected too much. These people had known me for only five years. The alumni paper of my alma mater is addressed to Jonetta Johnson. If I were the sensitive type I'd be a candidate for psychotherapy.

And that's not all. Someone almost killed my beloved cat, Rerun. Before an extended trip, I painstakingly researched all sorts of animal-care facilities in our area. My investigation resulted in the selection of a prestigious animal clinic in the Malibu Hills. Upon my return, I confidently drove to the facility and was greeted by what was left of my animal. Someone had forgotten to provide the advertised care. He neglected such "nonessential" items as food, water, bathing, and exercise. Just another example of nonexcellence!

Mastering the Art of Self-Destruction

To be fair, I must cease pointing my accusing finger at the rest of the world. My own life furnishes some remarkable examples of ineptitude: neglecting to preview a film for my church, a film that turned out to be risqué; wearing a wrong-color, wrong-style suit to a formal dinner at the Beverly Wilshire Hotel, and enduring those penetrating stares; tripping on the stage before thousands in the arena, and tens of thousands on television, just after receiving my Ph.D. diploma.

Many days I'm convinced that Murphy is my relative, maybe even my twin. Perhaps they also forgot to deliver him to my mother. You're familiar with his famous, constantly growing number of laws. Here are a few that I, especially, identify with:

The other line always moves faster.

The chance of the bread falling with the peanut-butter-and-jelly side down is directly proportionate to the cost of the carpet.

Any tool dropped while repairing a car will roll underneath to the exact center.

The repairman will never have seen a model quite like yours before.

You remember you forgot to take out the trash when the garbage truck is two doors away.

No matter how long or hard you shop for an item, after you've bought it, you'll find it on sale somewhere at a cheaper price.

Friends come and go, but enemies accumulate.

The light at the end of the tunnel is the headlamp of an oncoming train.[1]

Can you lay claim to being Murphy's kin? Or have you thought of instances of extreme ineptitude? If so, you will agree that excellence is needed in our day. Here we are speaking of secular excellence, excellence as a self-imposed standard of conduct. This means replacing bumbling with efficiency, carelessness with skill, embarrassment with pride.

In this day of technological sophistication, should not excellence characterize our society? The truth is, some people do excel, and in so doing become an inspiration for all of us.

The Few Whose Torches Are Lighted

Martin Luther King, Jr., was right: We *can* overcome, despite adversity, the trend toward mediocrity, and the temptation to rationalize our weaknesses. You simply cannot keep a good person down.

Cripple him, and you have a Sir Walter Scott. Lock him in a prison cell, and you have a John Bunyan.

Bury him in the snows of Valley Forge, and you have a George Washington.

Raise him in abject poverty, and you have an Abraham Lincoln.

Strike him down with infantile paralysis, and he becomes a Franklin D. Roosevelt.

Burn him so severely that the doctors say he'll never walk again, and you have a Glenn Cunningham—who set the world's one-mile record in 1934.

1. "Murphy's Law" (Millbrae, Calif.: Celestial Arts, 1979), quoted in Charles R. Swindoll, *Strengthening Your Grip: Essentials in an Aimless World* (Waco: Word, 1982), p. 211.

Deafen him and you have a Ludwig van Beethoven.

Have him or her born black in a society filled with racial discrimination, and you have a Booker T. Washington, a Marian Anderson, a George Washington Carver, or a Martin Luther King, Jr.

Call him a slow learner, "retarded," and write him off as uneducable, and you have an Albert Einstein.[2]

We see examples of excellence all around us. These persons, measuring themselves by themselves, set high standards. They know the fulfillment that accompanies attainment—whether it means playing the piano like Peter Nero or being a dependable custodian like Rosie Sanchez who cleans my office. These people, as Alfred North Whitehead would term it, "cultivate the habitual vision of greatness" every day.

Indefinable But Within Reach

Excellence is difficult to define. But we all certainly recognize it when we observe it in others. And we are refreshed and reassured when we witness it. What is excellence? It's a certain style of life, a manner of living, a bigness of spirit, a point of view, a frame of reference, a set of priorities, a hierarchy of values, an admirable self-imposed standard.[3]

As John W. Gardner says, we cannot "expect every man to be excellent. . . . But many more can achieve it than now do. Many, many more can try to achieve it than now do. And the society is bettered not only by those who achieve it but by those who are trying."[4]

Some people wince at the very mention of excellence.

2. Quoted in Ted W. Engstrom, *The Pursuit of Excellence* (Grand Rapids: Zondervan, 1982), p. 81.

3. C. William Fisher, *Our Goal Is Excellence* (Kansas City, Mo.: Beacon Hill, n.d.), p. 13.

4. John W. Gardner, *Excellence: Can We Be Equal and Excellent Too?* (New York: Harper and Row, 1961), p. 133.

Achieving excellence is like beginning a journey. To embark on this journey necessitates facing your painful weaknesses. Others begin the journey with the best of intentions, only to later succumb to the fatal disease of "unrealistic expectations." In some cases, these expectations were purposely placed beyond reach in order to cushion inevitable failure. Still others feign excellence, convincing more than a few. Their day of revelation approaches.

If only some of these disheartened ones could come to believe three truths.

First, every person, no matter how lowly, has the potential to attain excellence. In *Letters to His Son*, Lord Chesterfield writes, "There is scarcely anybody who is absolutely good for nothing, and hardly anybody good at everything."[5]

Second, involvement in the process of attaining excellence is intensely satisfying to the human spirit. Growth is its own reward; to cease growing is to start dying. On the inside cover of his Bible Oliver Cromwell had penned, *Qui cessat esse melior cessat esse bonus* (He who ceases to better ceases to be good).[6]

Third, excellence guarantees results! Attaining excellence is no empty ritual. Eventually it pays off. It improves individuals, but the ripple effect is also felt by all of society. Airplanes become safe. Clothes sent to the cleaners are returned cleaned. Restaurant food no longer tastes bland.

We're not speaking of forced excellence which Chrysler was made to resort to when the company was teetering on the brink of bankruptcy. Nor are we referring to the obsessive, workaholic-type excellence that reflects a sickness of mind and emotions.

Instead, we're speaking of a voluntary, flowing, con-

5. Quoted in Engstrom, *The Pursuit of Excellence*, p. 84.
6. Quoted in William Barclay, *The Daily Study Bible: The Letter to the Hebrews* (Philadelphia: Westminster, 1955), p. 52.

stantly improving excellence that corresponds with the rhythm of our nature. This is an excellence that strives for more than "getting by," that is concerned with "being" as well as "doing." It is an excellence that is within the reach of everyone from a large corporation like General Motors ("Ours is the way of excellence") to the Honda worker in Tokyo, who, on his lunch break, walks down the street straightening the windshield wipers on every parked Honda he encounters.[7]

If excellence is this great, why don't we hear more about it? Because we hear so much about success.

Aren't excellence and success the same? Many think so, but they are not. In fact, they are opposites in many respects. Not only that, but they are often enemies also. How is this so? I'm glad you asked.

7. Thomas J. Peters and Robert H. Waterman, Jr., *In Search of Excellence: Lessons from America's Best-Run Companies* (New York: Harper and Row, 1982), p. 37. On this same page, Peters and Waterman ask, "What exactly, is the nature of Japan's magic?" Then they quote *Fortune:* "The Japanese deserve credit for far more than the circumstantial triumph of being able to supply efficient cars to a country [the United States] caught short of them. They excel in the quality of fits and finishes, moldings that match, doors that don't sag, materials that look good and wear well, flawless paint jobs. Most important of all, Japanese cars have earned a reputation for reliability, borne out by the generally lower rate of warranty claims they experience. Technically, most Japanese cars are fairly ordinary."

The highest offices of the state and church resemble a pyramid whose top is accessible to only two sorts of animals—eagles and reptiles. —John Wesley

Since failure is our unforgiveable sin, we are willing to ignore all forms of deviance in people if they just achieve the success symbols which we worship.
—Anthony Campolo, *The Success Fantasy*

The pressure to succeed is greater than it has ever been. . . .People feel that they must pursue that goal even if it means crawling over the bodies of coworkers or sacrificing what they really want. —Paul Rosch, President, American Institute of Stress

2

Competing Ideals
Excellence and Success

John Mason Brown has written, "Existence is a strange bargain. Life owes us little; we owe it everything. The only true happiness comes from squandering ourselves for a purpose."[1]

Man's energies and creativity are mainly devoted to achieving two key purposes: excellence and success. There is usually some overlap. People who focus on one frequently attain a measure of the other. Again, we are speaking of excellence from a secular standpoint.[2] At this point

---

1. Quoted in John W. Gardner, *Excellence: Can We Be Equal and Excellent Too?* (New York: Harper and Row, 1961), p. 149.
2. It stands to reason that if a person excels, he is frequently successful. Also, the encouragement generated from being successful often motivates one increasingly to excel.

29

it might be helpful to examine both success and excellence. Such a comparison will provide a greater understanding of each.

Success: A Pot of Gold

For purposes of discussion, success is attaining cultural goals that are sure to elevate one's perceived importance within that culture. In practical terms, it means an elevation in power (having commands obeyed and wishes granted); privilege (being given special rights or favors); or wealth (accumulating financial reserves and the accompanying security).[3]

To a degree, every person is successful. But the term is mostly reserved for those who "have it made," or are "making it big." These people wear clothing with the right labels, eat at the best restaurants, and sit in the most expensive seats at the most exclusive social events. One person summarized the principle well: "Success is what your butcher would have if he were a surgeon."

Part of my wife's compensation as a travel consultant is in the form of passes to stay at resort hotels. One Christmas we stayed at one of Waikiki's newest and most prestigious hotels. We experienced a few days of lavish care fit for a V.I.P.

It began when our taxi pulled up to unload. A virtual army of attendants simultaneously opened all the car doors and the trunk. Bags disappeared in a flash. I still can't figure out how everyone knew our names without our telling them. No waiting at a registration desk for us! Instead, we were immediately escorted to the $220-per-night room. At our bedroom desk we quickly registered as we

---

3. Wealth, in this context, is both earned income and unearned gifts. In terms of status, the latter is more significant than the former. In the higher strata of society, "new money" is often perceived as unworthy of attention; instead, the family name gains one entrance.

consumed Swiss chocolates that had been delivered to our palatial quarters.

Tough life indeed! But one to which I, increasingly, found myself wanting to become accustomed. It was hard to pry away from such luxuries and begin living at home again, where there were no more chocolates on call or maids. The ultimate sacrifice was no more evening turndown of the bed—along with the accompanying pillow-gifts of a seashell and an orchid. Have I evoked your deepest sympathy?

I had status, and I loved it, even though, to use biblical language, it "came to pass" and was but "for a season."

Status is society telling you you've arrived, then treating you as if people believe it. No wonder people are driving themselves to achieve it! It beats scrubbing bathrooms, wearing rags, and waiting in welfare lines. A person has to be crazy to opt for noncomfort, unspecial treatment, an unspectacular existence.

Anthony Campolo, Jr., describes the extent to which success has captivated Americans:

> Success is a shining city, a pot of gold at the end of the rainbow. We dream of it as children, we strive for it through our adult lives, and we suffer melancholy in old age if we have not reached it.
>
> Success is the place of happiness. And the anxieties we suffer at the thought of not arriving there give us ulcers, heart attacks, and nervous disorders. If our reach exceeds our grasp, and we fail to achieve what we want, life seems meaningless and we feel emotionally dead.[4]

In a recent lead article in *People*, Brad Darrach poses the rhetorical question: "Why does the world's biggest crowd of celebrities pay millions for dime-size lots in a

---

4. Anthony Campolo, Jr., *The Success Fantasy* (Wheaton: Victor, 1980), p. 9.

perilous, polluted 'paradise?' "[5] The answer is obvious: for status. I know because I'm a professor at a university in Malibu—within a stone's throw from "the Colony," as it is called. I see the superrich as they leisurely stroll through the old-world shops—"dripping with gold jewelry" and purchasing whatever they desire. Cost is no consideration.

People affected by the "success fantasy" either live in places like Malibu, Beverly Hills, or Manhattan, or else constantly dream about it. They wish, hope, envy, or connive. Perhaps the last are the ones who should be most pitied. Their affections are set on an elusive dream.

How then does the motivation to succeed contrast with that to excel? What is the essential difference?

Excellence: The Rainbow

It is a well-known and accepted fact that our brain never really conceptualizes something until it contrasts that something with something else. For example, someone tells you that you're "pretty." Compared with what? Miss America? An orangutan? A person assures you that you're "smart." Compared with Albert Einstein, or a child in kindergarten? The last time I went to the dentist, I confidently declared that I had kept my mouth very clean. My dentist smiled and retorted, "Jon, a human's mouth is a virtual cesspool of germs—second only to that of a camel, in terms of filth." I thereafter revised my claim to say I maintain a clean mouth—compared with a camel's.

Similarly, our comprehension of excellence is enhanced by contrasting it with something we constantly hear about: success.

Please keep in mind that there is some overlap between the two. Also, I am not implying that one is invariably good and the other is always undesirable. Much depends on our motive. In addition, realize that there is little con-

5. Brad Darrach, "Malibu," *People*, 1 August 1983, p 51.

sensus among those who have attempted to define these concepts. Therefore, I am taking the liberty to furnish my own definitions. The following are the differences that *I* perceive. Finally, once again remind yourself that we are speaking of these ideals from a secular point of view, although there are obvious spiritual overtones.

Success offers a hoped-for future goal.

Excellence provides a striven-for present standard.

Success bases our worth on a comparison with others.

Excellence gauges our value by measuring us against our own potential.

Success grants its rewards to the few, but is the dream of the multitudes.

Excellence is available to all living beings, but is accepted by the special few.

Success focuses its attention on the external—becoming the tastemaker for the insatiable appetites of the conspicuous consumer.

Excellence beams its spotlight on the internal spirit—becoming the quiet, but pervasive, conscience of the conscientious who yearn for integrity.

Success engenders fantasy and a compulsive groping for the pot of gold at the end of the rainbow.

Excellence brings us to reality, and a deep gratitude for the affirming promise of the rainbow.

Success encourages expedience and compromise, which prompt us to treat people as means to our ends.

Excellence cultivates principles and consistency, which ensure that we will treat all persons as intrinsically valuable ends—the apex of our heavenly Father's creation.

It is evident that success pales in the brilliance of excellence. The latter, in comparison with the former, is an essential ingredient in the character of any nation. To possess it is to survive and to continually improve. To lack it is to at best merely exist and to inevitably shrink to a deplorable nothingness.

Therefore, in our world, excellence must not be perceived as optional. It is a necessity. The same cannot be said for success. Even perishing societies have successful people. But, lacking excellence, their fate is sealed.

Excellence is always expensive—whether in a house, car, rocket, or mousetrap. It is never on sale. Those who attain excellence must pay the full cost. That often means enduring those kinds of rejection that inevitably accompany falling out of rank in the world's parade in order to march with few to the beat of another drummer. But excellence is well worth the sacrifice. It is far more valuable than any form of fleeting success.

The poet James Russell Lowell provides words that beautifully summarize this principle:

> Life is a leaf of paper white
> Whereon each one of us may write
> His word or two,
> And then comes night.
>
> Greatly begin, though thou have time
> But for a line,
> Be that sublime,
> *Not failure, but low aim, is crime.*[6]

---

6. Quoted in Ted W. Engstrom, *The Pursuit of Excellence* (Grand Rapids: Zondervan, 1982), p. 92.

Excellent things are rare. — Plato, *The Republic*

. . . it seems to me, each individual amongst us could in his own person, with the utmost grace and versatility prove himself self-sufficient in the most varied forms of activity. — Pericles, funeral oration

He who knows Palestine and Greece knows the germ of four-fifths or more of western civilization, and has seen its animating and sustaining forces in their simplest and purest forms. — R. W. Livingstone, *Greek Ideals and Modern Life*

Athens, the source whence civilization, knowledge, religion, agriculture, justice, and law have sprung and spread into all lands. — Cicero

3

The Greeks Had a Word for It

He grimaces with pain. Veins protrude in his neck. Every leg muscle strains to the limit. His lungs feel like they're in flames. The sprinter, who has trained arduously for this moment of truth, suddenly spurts ahead of the other runners and crosses the finish line with a final burst of energy. He has won the race, but receives no gold medal, only a simple garland cut with a golden sickle. He climbs no victor's platform to accept the crowd's acclaim. Instead, he bows at a nearby shrine, dedicated to his warrior god, Zeus, to offer a quiet prayer of gratitude.

The year is 776 B.C. The place is the sacred plain of Olympia.

Almost three millennia later, I stood with my university students beside the ruins of the ancient track. Our guide, Olympia's mayor, provided a vivid mental journey into the past:

> The Games were, primarily, worship rituals to honor the gods of Greek mythology. That is why the premises were crowded with altars, statues, and sacred mounds.[1]

> No women were allowed among the twenty thousand spectators. Any discovered were put to death.[2]

> Runners wore no clothes, and even greased down their bodies to reduce wind resistance.

> Just prior to the Games, nobles from Elis journeyed to all Greek cities to proclaim *ekecheiria,* a cessation of all hostilities for a period of three months.

As he dramatized, I couldn't help contrasting the scene he described with the Olympics of our day. Certainly the ancient Greeks weren't concerned with boycotts, drug tests, television by satellite, bribery, hostage seizing, or asylum seeking.

Admittedly, participants desired to win, but not in order to declare, "Hey, world, look what I did!" They did not

1. This was originally a religious shrine, dedicated to exalting the gods and honoring the deceased. At the Great Altar of Zeus the accumulated ashes of the sacrificed animals gradually formed a seven-meter-high mound. The sacred flame burned within the Enclosure of Zeus, a circle of upright slabs, where an oracle spoke through the movements of the sacrificial bull's skin. *Touring Greece* (Athens: Editions K. Gouvoussis, n.d.), pp. 63–67. Apart from the Great Altar of Zeus, where the richest sacrifices were offered, there were many altars. Pausanias mentions sixty-nine. Manolis Andronicos, *Olympia* (Athens: Ekdotike Athenon S.A., n.d.), p. 6.

2. There was one exception to this rule. One beauty queen, representative of the gods, was allowed to witness the events. She was given all the privileges of a high-school homecoming queen.

hope to receive a call from the country's president, nor to land a seven-figure-salary professional contract.[3]

What motivated the ancient Olympic athletes? What drove them toward sacrificial preparation during the years of their youth? To willingly accept long hours of training in the scorching Mediterranean sun?

The All-Consuming Ambition

One obsession burned within the breast of all Olympic competitors—namely, the yearning for authentic excellence. Excellence was more precious, it was thought, than costly gems, wealth, or unbounded power.

What held true for these athletes was a reality for other walks of life: philosophers like Aristotle; savage fighters like Diomede; poverty-stricken peasants like Hesiod; even Athenian youth who flocked to sophists in order to be guided toward the ideal.

It was the intentional aim of the ancient Greek society to achieve excellence, in spite of the fact that the culture was steeped in superstition. Is it any wonder that excellence has been termed the "instinct of the Greek race" or that it is discussed in the earliest literature of that ancient civilization? Plato gave much thought to it, as did Homer and most other authors. The ideal of achieving excellence was the very cornerstone of ancient Hellenic society.

3. The Games took place under the gaze and protection of the warrior god Zeus, according to Greek legend. He was believed to be the one who always stood by the Hellenes, whether in the struggles of war or in the peaceful athletic contests. In return, the Greeks, being a deeply religious people, offered him the arms which had brought them victory and the spoils of war which the god had helped them appropriate. All victors set up their own statues in the shrine of Zeus, not out of arrogance, but with the piety of those who can accept a god's gift in perfect humility. As the years went by, the votive offerings in the sacred grove grew so numerous that they could be numbered in the thousands. They included precious and famed trinkets of war and games that resulted in Olympia becoming the most complete museum of Greek history. Andronicos, *Olympia*, p. 16.

Today we're quite impressed by the concept of excellence, which most dictionaries define as superiority. We smile when our boss tells us that we have performed in an excellent manner or when the coach says we have excelled. And who hasn't seen movies about European kings who were addressed by the pompous title *Your Excellency?*

We have a pretty good idea of what we mean by excellence. But what exactly did the Greeks mean when they used the word? Did they mean what we mean or something more?

Arete: The Ultimate's Ultimate

Words can be mighty. "Freedom" has been the rally cry for many wars, as have "Fatherland" and "destiny." But few words in the annals of history have carried the richness of meaning of *aretē,* the Greek term for excellence. In some contexts it suggests "virtue"; in others "superiority"; in still others "preeminence" and even "perfection."[4]

Think of the ultimate of which mankind is capable. Then, add still more because of the limitation of your mind. Now you have but a shadowy idea of the concept's meaning.

R. W. Livingstone's understanding of *aretē* is illuminating:

> It is the belief that man is more important than his environment or his possessions, and that his fundamental business is not to understand nature, though this is one of his problems, nor to earn a livelihood, though that is one of his duties, but so to lead his life as to [attain] . . . all of what is characteristic of, peculiar to, and highest in human nature; or, as the Greeks put it, to achieve the *arete* of man.[5]

4. R. W. Livingstone, *Greek Ideals and Modern Life* (London: Oxford University Press, n.d.), pp. 69–72.
5. Ibid., p. 88.

An inspiring concept to be sure, and one that the ancient Greeks were driven to attain. But why? What is the magnetic appeal of excellence? Just what was it about this ideal that was considered so inviting and rejuvenating?

To put it simply, the contemplation of *aretē* had a way of generating awesome power for the ancient Greeks. It had power to draw men away from lesser aims to follow after it. The best, when conceptualized, was desired and sought. To realize that man had a perfection generated creative and energetic activity. As one author put it: "The mere idea of human perfection constituted a self-evident claim on the human spirit."[6]

The concept had power to develop from lower to higher conceptions of good, in a vision that was progressively purified and enlarged as human experience grew. There was nothing fixed nor static in *aretē!* The ideal grew as the intellect grew and rose as high as the imagination could take it.

Aretē also had power to broaden perspective so that narrowness and provincialism vanished. Unlike most societies, which are afflicted by the "prison of the tribal, and the intellectual tyranny of the contemporary,"[7] ancient Greeks saw life as life—with all of its diversities, dimensions, and complexities.

Finally, the concept had power to attract men to the inherent value of itself. It was addictive. When authentic excellence was seen in all of its radiant beauty, it became its own reward. Rather than being primarily valued for its products—be they wealth, architecture, or Olympic victory—excellence was prized for itself. Involvement in the process of attaining it became intensely gratifying. This feeling is evident in these lines:

6. Ibid., p. 77.
7. This phrase is often used in anthropology to single out the two manifestations of the stereotype-prejudice-discrimination syndrome, which leads to ethnocentrism. These manifestations are relinquishing individuality to group goals, and basing all values, norms, and status on present-day tastes and fads.

How good is man's life, the mere living!
How fit to employ all the soul and the mind
and the senses for ever in joy![8]

Aretē generated spectacular accomplishments among
the ancient Greeks. In addition, their excellence produced
an awesome effect.

The Lingering Legacy

The Greek civilization became, without a doubt, the
most admired and imitated of all of human history.

Hear Johann Wolfgang von Goethe as he declares, "Of
all peoples the Greeks have dreamt of life best."[9] Or Percy
Bysshe Shelley as he says, "What we are and hope to be
is derived from the influence and inspiration of these glorious generations."[10] Or Alexander von Humboldt as he
states, "No other people has combined simplicity and naturalness with so high a culture. The state of Athens at its
climax, that is of human nature at its climax."[11]

Because we are so product-oriented, our admiration is
mainly directed toward the Greeks' physical creations: the
philosophical and scientific writings; the intricately carved
statues from which Michelangelo took his cues; the clas-
sic architecture, which is the model for the facades of our
courthouses.

As impressive as these are, the ancient Hellenic legacy
provides mankind with an even greater gift, a profound
perspective which fascinates the imagination and kindles
the soul—the ideal of excellence. To fully grasp this view
of life is to experience true renaissance, regardless of the
spatial or temporal setting.

When we realize this fact, crucial questions come to

8. Livingstone, *Greek Ideals and Modern Life*, p. 79.
9. Quoted, ibid., p. 43.
10. Ibid.
11. Ibid.

mind: How did the Greek ideal of excellence filter into God's Word? In what ways was its meaning altered?

Let's focus on answers to these important questions.

Part **2**

Excellence
Norm of God's Word

Let us thank God that he makes us live among the present problems. . . . It is no longer permitted to anyone to be mediocre. — Pope Pius XI

A Christian should constantly seek . . . highest standards and employ the most demanding comparisons for [his self-] evaluations. — J. Richard Chase

It is particularly significant that Christ's people, who have tasted immortal knowledge, serve him with excellence. — J. Kenneth Grider

The early Christian church conquered because the Christians of those days out-thought, out-lived, and out-died the pagans. — T. R. Glover

4

Understanding with Open Mind

It's amusing to watch foreigners try to communicate when they can't speak the language. The same few words are loudly repeated over and over in an unintelligible accent and with plenty of vigorous hand motions.

As a traveler to a distant land, it is awkward to be forced to use such tactics. But it would seem even more difficult if you were attempting to converse with foreigners in your homeland, especially when such aliens are considered intruders by your closest friends!

Jesus found himself in such a situation. He no doubt came into frequent contact with Greeks and Greek-speaking Jews. After all, his boyhood town of Nazareth was but two miles south of Sepphoris, the "all-Greek" capital of Herod Antipas.

45

Our Lord may have belonged to a family and community of Jews who tenaciously clung to their Jewishness. Nevertheless, such people must have been like an island in a sea of Greek customs and ideas. It is possible that our Lord spoke a broken Greek—similar to a Tijuana shopkeeper's broken English. Certainly he was fully aware of the impact of Greek thinking on Jewish life.[1]

That influence had deeply penetrated Israel. Three centuries had passed since the days when the greatest of all Greek commanders, Alexander, had invaded and conquered its land (332 B.C.). That same influence lasted about another six centuries, until the time of the Arab takeover (A.D. 636).[2]

After enduring Jewish rejection, it is little wonder that Jesus increasingly directed his ministry to the Greeks. He journeyed to their cities: Bethsaida, Caesarea Philippi, and the coastal town of Tyre, as well as the great cities (Decapolis) near the Sea of Galilee. This ministry intensified until the Jews reacted with anger, seeing him much as a Klansman might see a Mississippi white man who accepted a black man's invitation to dinner.

Following Christ's example, the early church continued

1. Although his archaeological focus has been near the Sea of Galilee, primarily at Tel Hum (Capernaum), John Wilson states that first-century Jewish graves throughout the entire region are inscribed in Greek. His point: The language people think in is, as an archaeological rule, the language they select for their tombstones. Wilson's observation about Palestine also holds true for the first-century Jews buried in foreign lands. "The dominant position of Greek among the Jews of the Diaspora may be seen from a study of catacomb inscriptions from Rome, which shows that seventy-four percent were in Greek, twenty-four percent in Latin, and only two percent in Hebrew or Aramaic." Harry J. Leon, *The Jews of Rome* (Philadelphia: Jewish Publication Society, 1961), quoted in Donald J. Wiseman and Edwin Yamauchi, *Archaeology and the Bible: An Introductory Study* (Grand Rapids: Zondervan, 1979), p. 66. The influence of Greek thinking on Christ's world must have been great and related to all areas.

2. Although the zionistic Maccabees successfully expunged the land of foreigners (160 B.C.), even they remained Greek in language and thought. The rule of Roman Caesars, Herods, and governors (47 B.C. onward) was likewise Hellenistic.

to focus attention on Greeks. When it came time to pen his inspired letters to the churches, Paul wrote in Greek— because he was writing mostly to Greeks. Although Paul sought to reach both Jews and Greeks, he discovered among cosmopolitan Greeks a far greater potential for spreading the gospel than among the Hebrews.

But what about the Greek words that Paul and other biblical writers used? Words that we believe to be inspired and inspiring? Words that we live by? Are the meanings of such Greek words tainted by pagan Greek philosophy?

Biblical authors, guided by God's Spirit, added to Greek concepts and words a new dimension.[3] One such word is *aretē*, Greek for "excellence." As we have noted, the ancient Greeks accorded the concept great significance, so that the effort to attain to excellence became the virtual bedrock of their civilization. The word referred to the ultimate of what is characteristic of or peculiar to the highest in human nature. The ancient Greeks believed that the greatest manifestation of excellence is possessing profound wisdom. For wisdom, the queen of the virtues, is the gateway to the good, the true, the beautiful.

This is impressive, perhaps even awesome, when you think of what the concept helped the Greeks accomplish. But the writers of God's Word used *aretē* to describe other concepts and qualities. Excellence became intimately associated with the daily Christian walk. Christians were

3. A prime illustration of this is the Greek word *logos*, which implied truth, logic, and symmetry. Ancient Greeks placed the word in the context of an abstract, philosophical idea upon which the world existed. New Testament writers expanded the term to mean the living, dynamic person of Jesus Christ, who embodies all the Greeks meant and much more (John 1:1–5). Another example is *pistis*, the Greek word for faith. Whether used narrowly as a philosophical term, or in the vernacular, it suggested a man-generated confidence based on trust in his own abilities. Biblical authors employed the term to mean a deep trust based on the abiding assurance that our Lord strengthens us from within (Heb. 11; 12:2; 1 Peter 1:5). He is the Vine. We are the branches that draw sustenance from the Vine (John 15:5). As a result, we can be sure that our fruit-bearing potential is as limitless as his inexhaustible power and infinite wisdom.

given a motivating, enriching, but attainable standard providing full access to the victorious life.

The Metamorphosis of a Concept

What, then, does excellence—as it is described in the Bible—mean for the Christian?

Influential Christian scholars and leaders replied to this question in a recent survey that I administered. Their answers are enlightening.

> Following out to its end the intrinsic character of a quality, event, or mode of being, and seeing this pursuit in light of . . . the resurrection—that all things cohere in Christ.—Martin Marty

> Doing all to the glory of God, which requires my best.—Hudson Armerding

> Discovering who we are as Christ's people, and committing ourselves to live out his radical servant lifestyle within the body of Christ.—Larry Richards

> There is no such thing as Christian excellence, just as there is no Christian hamburger; but a Christian will strive for excellence (i.e., integrity) with every task he attempts. It could mean making the very best hamburger you can—with plenty of onion, tomato, and pickle.—Haddon Robinson

> Wholism, or seeing the whole of life as subject to the lordship of Jesus Christ; may be at the core of Christian excellence. And at the center of such wholism is wholesomeness.—David Moberg

All of these definitions focus on important elements of what excellence means for the Christian: glorifying God, being servants, seeing things in light of the resurrection, having integrity, and being wholistic and wholesome in attitude. Thus, "excellence" is an umbrella term. That is why *aretē* is translated "virtue," a general term, in addition to "excellence."

But it must be understood that the most important dimension of excellence is *agapē* love, the supreme virtue. Mark Moore put it well: "It is as we improve the expression of God-given love that we come to realize the standard of Christian excellence."

Paul declares, "And now these three [cardinal virtues] remain: faith, hope and love. But the greatest of these is (*agapē*) love" (1 Cor. 13:13). Perhaps that is because, as J. Kenneth Grider states, "Of the three, only love will not cease in the next world." Or, as has also been suggested, maybe love is a summation of all the other virtues.

This same thirteenth chapter of First Corinthians is universally known as the "love chapter" of God's Word. Generations have received instruction and inspiration from its wise and uplifting thoughts. Without a doubt, it is a Gibralter of our faith. It is important to note that Paul's profound teaching on the supremacy of love is introduced with words that clearly reveal an inseparable link between excellence and love: "And now I [Paul] will show you the most excellent way" (1 Cor. 12:31). What is it? The way of love.[4]

The Bible is emphatic. If we desire excellence—the kind of excellence that will bring the most glory to our heavenly Father—we must deepen in our understanding of, and commitment to, authentic *agapē* love, a love that is unconditional, sacrificial, and available to all.

---

4. Equating excellence with *agapē* love is this author's understanding of the connoted definition of *aretē*. Theologians-exegetes Ralph Earle, W. T. Purkiser, and J. Kenneth Grider, when queried, concurred with this understanding. Although biblical excellence is not only *agapē* love, it is the latter in its most refined sense. W. E. Vine provides a denotated definition: "Arete properly denotes whatever procures pre-eminent estimation for a person or thing; hence, intrinsic eminence, moral goodness, virtue, (a) of God . . . (b) of any particular moral excellence . . . where virtue is enjoined as an essential quality in the exercise of faith." W. E. Vine, *An Expository Dictionary of New Testament Words* (Old Tappan, N.J.: Revell, 1966), pp. 189–190.

Available to all. Now there's an inspiring thought! What a contrast to the excellence of the ancient Greeks: excellence equated with great powers of reason. That excellence would be restricted to the few born with an extraordinary mind and having had the opportunity to develop it.[5] By contrast, Christian excellence is within everyone's reach: philosopher and artist, but also the illiterate and impoverished; gold medalists and people who never get to be first in anything. An overflowing, unpretentious, and genuine love can be possessed by even the most obscure and insignificant persons. In fact, Christ's Sermon on the Mount seems to say that such people are closer to such love than those of great power and wealth (Matt. 5:3–11).

Christian excellence is *agapē* love. But what else is said about excellence in God's Word?

5. To illustrate, according to Aristotle, several conditions must be present before *aretē* can exist. He states, "Evidently it [i.e., *aretē*] needs external goods as well; for it is impossible or not easy to do what is noble unless furnished with external means. There are many things that can only be done through the instrumentality of friends or wealth or political power; and there are some things, such as good birth, good looks and good children, the lack of which take the lustre from happiness." Thus, to the Greek, *aretē* required more than a usual endowment of intelligence. That intelligence had to be cultivated or developed with the support of such ideal conditions. If one is aware of this and other radical contrasts between ancient Greek and biblical concepts of excellence, it is understandable that some scholars would overreact by opposing all Greek ideas in God's Word. Such was the position of Rudolf Bultmann and other liberal German theologians who held that all that Jesus said is good, but all other biblical instruction is tainted by Greek influence (e.g., doctrine of the Trinity). According to this view, the Greeks, who pervasively appeared on the scene after Christ's death, brought distortion and error. As a result, their additions ruined the original Semitic simplicity of Holy Writ. Therefore we cannot legitimately accept the Book of Acts and other Scripture that has been infiltrated by their heretical thoughts. On the surface, this position may appear plausible. However, on closer inspection, it is accurately seen as a baseless rationalization providing license to reject inspired sections of our Bible. As Wilson states, "Christianity was *always* a form of Hellenistic Judaism. There was no abrupt movement from Jewishness to Greekness." With this in mind, we are justified in accepting the totality of Scripture with clear conscience and sound reason.

The Source and Supplier of Excellence: God

Excellence describes the very nature of God. The psalmist declared, "How excellent is thy name [i.e., nature] in all the earth" (8:1, KJV).[6]

Furthermore, the excellence of our heavenly Father is closely intertwined with his glory. The Hebrew word for "glory" (hod), in reference to God, is translated aretē by writers of the Septuagint (see Hab. 3:3; Zech. 6:13). The scholars believed that our Creator's glory is best described by the Greek word for excellence.

So we can conclude that God's glory is his excellence! And his excellence is his glory. Not incidentally, that is closely related to the Bible's straightforward statement that "God is love" (1 John 4:7), the divine embodiment of true excellence.

We find ourselves asking how we, who are plagued with so many inglorious frailities and limitations, can meaningfully relate to the glorious, excellent one.

"Where He Leads" is a favorite hymn of mine—especially the fourth stanza which asserts, "He will give me grace and glory."[7] It is wonderful to know that God is excellent and glorified, but to know that he will share excellence with us is no less than inspiring. How is this possible? Because he is the supreme wellspring of grace and glory, we know that these gifts are his to give. To discover that his glory and excellence are inseparable is to treasure the song's words and his generous gift, even more.

Reflect on this a moment. Rather than hoarding his radiant excellence, our God lovingly offers to bestow it upon us, his rebellious and undeserving creation. It is with

6. In Hebrew society, and throughout most cultures of the ancient world, a person's name was thought to connote his identity. Hence, upon his conversion, the name Saul was changed to "Paul." When we are told that God's name is Excellence, we realize that this means his entire nature is permeated with excellence.

7. John S. Norris and E. W. Blandly, Worship in Song (Kansas City, Mo.: Lilleanas, 1972), p. 397.

good reason that Peter triumphantly declares, "For His divine power has bestowed upon us every requisite for life and goodness, through knowing Him who called us to His own glory and excellence" (2 Peter 1:3, NBV). This is excellence that defies adequate description and stretches our imaginations.

In sharp contrast, the Greeks believed that excellence was based on the sheer efforts of man. Through his own efforts, man could fashion an elaborate ethical system that would enable him to develop his potential. As he plodded along on his path toward excellence he might eventually discover some mysterious, impersonal god-source. But he shouldn't count on it. For the ancient Greeks, the journey toward excellence began with the visible and moved toward the invisible; from humanity to deity.

This is not so with Christian excellence. God's Word assures us of more than a hope in finding our Maker at the end of the road—provided we have attained excellence. Instead, we can know that the Father of all excellence—whose nature and will are revealed to all who have receptive hearts—joins us at the beginning of our journey toward excellence. With each step he provides strength for the next one.

What are the results of his excellence in our lives?

Thoughts That Soothe and Comfort

As we open the doors of our hearts (see Rev. 3:20) to receive divine excellence, we find ourselves yearning to apply that gift to every area of our life.

Such application begins with a radical purging of our minds. Unclean thoughts must go. Jesus once declared that evil thoughts proceed from the heart (Matt. 15:19). This implies that as our hearts are filled with his love, our thoughts will become pure.

God's Word proclaims that we are judged, in part, by the thoughts and attitudes of our hearts (Heb. 4:12). Why are thoughts so crucial? They are the prelude to attitudes, words, actions.

Paul instructed all believers with these words: "whatever is true, whatever is noble, whatever is right, whatever is pure, whatever is lovely, whatever is admirable—if anything is excellent or praiseworthy—think about such things" (Phil. 4:8).

Excellence in thought is urgently needed today, when scores are burdened with a punishing self-image, the evening news is saturated with stories about blood and tragedy, and video shops blatantly peddle mind-polluting pornography, often featuring sadism and masochism. In short, we're constantly bombarded with the opposite of the true, noble, right, pure, lovely, admirable—those virtues that Paul admonishes us to meditate upon.

With the excellent One's help, we must and will swim upstream in our evil world, although the water is swift and treacherous as well as polluted. We will intentionally fill our minds with his thoughts and purposes. Then our lives will take on revitalized meaning. Our perspectives will be healthy, positive, hopeful. After all, we are "a chosen people, a royal priesthood, a holy nation, a people belonging to God . . . declar[ing] the praises of him who called [us] out of darkness into his wonderful light" (1 Peter 2:9).

It is not enough to have minds that radiate with his excellence. That same excellence must characterize our actions. We must be constantly involved in loving deeds.

Acting on Intentions

Someone said, "After all is said and done, there's a lot more said than done." After attaining to excellent thoughts, we must do what we know we must do.

What T. H. Huxley said about education is true concerning Christian excellence. To paraphrase: It motivates us to do what we should do, when it should be done, as it should be done, whether it is convenient or not.

The Epistle of James has a lot to say about "doing" excellence. The author poses a penetrating question: "What good is it, my brothers, if a man claims to have faith but has no deeds?" (2:14). His answer: "Faith by itself, if it is not accompanied by action, is dead" (2:17). "Show me your faith without deeds, and I will show you my faith by what I do" (2:18b). On a more somber note he warns, "Anyone, then, who knows the good he ought to do and doesn't do it, sins" (4:17).

In his checklist of things to be done by every true disciple of Christ, Peter instructs, "Make every effort to add to your faith goodness (aretē; 2 Peter 1:5). Why? "For if you do these things, you will never fall, and you will receive a rich welcome into the eternal kingdom of our Lord and Savior Jesus Christ" (1:10b–11).

Excellent deeds reflect the very nature and character of our excellent God. They're not optional for the Christian; they are standard. But what kinds of excellent deeds?

First, there are deeds of preparation. These are the actions that ready us for the ongoing, challenging race we must run against the forces of evil.

Ancient Olympians trained for a full year prior to the Games. Arduous discipline and abstinence characterized their life during this critical period. Philostratus the Elder advised, "If you have worked hard enough to render yourself worthy of . . . Olympia, if you have not been idle or ill-disciplined, then go with confidence; but those who have not trained in this fashion, let them go where they will."

The Christian race—which is like a marathon—demands no less. Paul captures the spirit when he says, "I beat my body and make it my slave so that . . . I myself will not be disqualified for the prize" (1 Cor. 9:27). Employing the same analogy, the writer to the Hebrews admonishes us to "throw off everything that hinders and the sin that so easily entangles, [so that we can] run with perseverance the race marked out for us" (12:1).

"Beat my body," "throw off everything that hinders"—
these are words of action. They are words that imply discipline. However, it is a discipline grounded in love and
hope, the kind possessed by America's late Olympic hero,
Jesse Owens, who endured years of rigorous training to
attain victory at the Berlin Games. His athletic excellence
stunned the world, inciting spectator Adolf Hitler to storm
out of the stadium in a rage. Was his accomplishment
worth the sacrifice? Ask any patriotic American.

Our deeds of preparation for God's race must reflect
deep dedication and intense love—the appropriate response to the One who offered (John 3:16) and continues
to offer his best. But God makes our preparation satisfying, reminding us that we too will some day "have our
Munich" as Satan witnesses our victory and his defeat!

But what about the race itself? A second kind of good
deeds must emerge: deeds that serve others so that they
will come to recognize God's love. Robert Murray Mc-
Cheyne said it well: "A Christian is [one whose deeds]
make it easy for others to believe in God." What is implied? On one hand, our deeds must not offend. But our
servantlike deeds must also intersect human need—in the
name of the One who commanded us to give "cup[s] of
cold water" (Matt. 10:42).

James provides a helpful list of examples:

persevere under trial (1:12)

be quick to listen and slow to anger (1:19)

refrain from showing favoritism (2:1)

care for the physical needs of others (2:15–18)

tame the tongue (3:7–8)

avoid fighting (4:1), adultery (4:4; i.e., "friendship with
   the world"), self-indulgence (5:5), grumbling against
   another, and swearing (5:12)

help those who have wandered from the truth (5:19–20)

These are running skills for the Christian marathoner who manifests excellence. They are fundamentals but are often neglected in our life.

How often I have neglected some of these essentials in the heat of my race! Continuing to hope for success, I've allowed opportunities to do excellent deeds to slip away. As a result, I've found myself doing such defeating things as jumping the gun (showing impatience), dropping the baton (betraying trust), pulling a hamstring (developing crippling guilt), and obeying the crowd (conforming). Have you ever succumbed to these temptations?

Failure in the Christian race is serious. If you lose the mile run in the Olympics, you and your friends are hurt. But mediocre deeds in life's race affect the many that could be led away from suffering and toward our God of love.

But if divinely endowed, self-giving, and unconditional *agape* love can give us loving thoughts and motivate us to do loving deeds, how can we attain it? How can we become incarnations of his love?

This One's by Invitation Only

An awareness of God's generous offer to provide us with an unlimited quantity of love is important. But it is not sufficient to bring it to pass. In addition, we must consciously choose to invite him into our lives. He comes by invitation. How do we go about inviting his excellence and gift of love?

First, we invite him through sincere confession. Past sins are to be acknowledged. After expressing a genuine sorrow, we must ask God to take them away (2 Cor. 7:10; Acts 17:30). This is followed by a promise to do an about-face—to begin the new life of love (2 Cor. 5:17; Eph. 4:22–24). Finally, we must accept by faith that we are forgiven (Rom. 10:9–10). Such faith is grounded on the promise of God's infallible Word. Thanks to the sacrifice of Jesus on the cross we know with assurance that "if we confess our sins, he is faithful and just and will forgive us our sins and purify us from all unrighteousness" (1 John 1:9).

When we have confessed in faith, the Holy Spirit confirms the truth of the experience in our hearts (Rom. 8:16–17). As a result, we know without doubt that we've been born again. We are pardoned rebels.

Second, at a subsequent time we invite him through complete consecration. This is a time when we surrender our will to his will. Such consecration is thorough and complete. It was what Paul wished for the Thessalonians when he declared, "May God himself, the God of peace, sanctify you through and through. May your whole spirit, soul and body be kept blameless at the coming of our Lord Jesus Christ" (1 Thess. 5:23).[8]

Our heavenly Father has provided for this second work of grace, commonly referred to as entire sanctification.[9] In receiving this grace, our sinful nature is instanta-

8. One person suggested that *through and through* calls to mind the image of a piece of inlaid linoleum, whose color is the same from top to bottom. It is clear that in this verse, Paul is admonishing entire sanctification on those who had already confessed their sins and become born again. He continually thanks God for them (1:2), remembers their "work produced by faith," their "labor prompted by love," their "endurance inspired by hope" (1:3), refers to them as "brothers loved by God" who had been "chosen" (1:4), "imitators of us and of the Lord; in spite of severe suffering" (1:6), and "a model to all the believers in Macedonia and Achaia" (1:7). He declares that he thanks God because they "received the word of God" and "accepted it" fully (2:13). The Thessalonians were forgiven sinners! Nevertheless, the apostle beckons them to the second work of grace, namely, entire sanctification.

9. Other terms for the consecration are heart holiness, baptism of the Holy Spirit, second blessing, fullness of the Spirit. Entire sanctification is this author's preference because it can be linked with initial sanctification, which takes place in confession. Both are sanctification. Both are works of the Holy Spirit. But one focuses on the forgiveness of past sins and the other directs attention to the cleansing of our sinful nature. The so-called Holiness churches of our world boldly proclaim the doctrine of entire sanctification. They trace lineage to John Wesley, James Arminius, the Reformers, the church fathers, and biblical authors. It was John Wesley, however, who particularly popularized the teaching, making it the cornerstone doctrine of the Methodist church.

neously cleansed.[10] Our original sin (in contrast to past
sins that are forgiven in confession), which we inherited
from Adam, is completely removed. We are purged of all
uncleanness. More than pardoned rebels, we become intimate, obedient children of God—his transformed creation (Rom. 12:1–2).

When such a dramatic event takes place in our life,
important results are purity of heart (Acts 15:8–9) and
power to witness (Acts 1:8).

In terms of love/excellence, we're readied for life's race.

10. According to J. Kenneth Grider, John Wesley and Holiness-movement
writers teach that entire sanctification is instantaneous. Nevertheless, Wesley
also perceived a gradual element in the second blessing as original sin is mor-
tified. Some Holiness-movement writers employ progressive sanctification
terms referring to a gradual preparation of the mind and heart for the all-at-
once cleansing. Grider proceeds to offer five biblical bases for teaching that
original sin is instantaneously cleansed in entire sanctification. *It is a baptism.*
John the Baptist proclaimed that Jesus would baptize with the Holy Spirit
(Matt. 3:11). This occurred in the hearts of the disciples on the day of Pentecost. Then Christ's prayer, "sanctify them" (John 17:17), was answered. Their
hearts were purified (Acts 15:9). Baptism occurs at a point in time. A person
cannot be partially baptized and later fully baptized. Likewise, there is no
gradual spiritual purification. Original sin is expelled, destroyed, cleansed at
one stroke. *It is a sealing.* Three times in the New Testament (2 Cor. 1:22;
Eph. 1:13; 4:30) "sealing" is a symbol of entire sanctification. It suggests God's
ownership and approval of our lives. And it suggests instantaneousness. A
person could not keep on sealing a letter with hot wax. *It is a circumcision.*
Circumcision is analogous to entire sanctification (see Col. 2:11, NASB). Paul
is saying that the "body of the flesh" is circumcised. The state, condition, or
principle of the flesh is cut away. And this, too, is not a more-and-more matter.
It is received by faith. If it were by works, then it would be gradual only,
never becoming complete or fully obtained. But entire sanctification, like justification, comes by faith (Acts 15:8–9; 26:18). Although faith might suggest
an extended quality, faith as the means of obtainment suggests that any con-
secrated believer may, at any instant, exercise the kind of believing trust which
results in God's grace of entire sanctification. *The aorist tense.* The verbal
cognates of *hagiazō* (sanctify) suggest instantaneousness. The word, in its verbal forms, appears twenty-eight times in the New Testament. It is in the aorist
tense twelve times, in the perfect tense seven times, and in the present tense
nine times. The aorist tense, the most common one in the Greek, appears in
numerous other words relating to entire sanctification. *Entire Sanctification:
The Distinctive Doctrine of Wesleyanism* (Kansas City, Mo.: Beacon Hill,
1980), pp. 91–97.

Agape love filters down into the deepest recesses of our heart. Not only are sin's symptoms removed (as with consecration), but the poisonous virus of evil is eradicated from our life's blood stream. The purity of divine love flows within. We have a clean bill of spiritual health!

In addition, we are empowered with a wisdom and boldness to effectively spread the Good News of Christ's love to others. Jesus realized this and thought about the need for his disciples to witness with excellence. After he had instituted the Lord's Supper, he fervently prayed to God for their complete consecration: "They are not of the world, even as I am not of it. Sanctify [Greek *hagiazō,* make holy] them by the truth; your word is truth. As you sent me into the world, I have sent them into the world. For them I sanctify myself, that they too may be truly sanctified" (John 17:16–19).

Our Lord's prayer was no doubt answered on the day of Pentecost, when his disciples were filled with the Holy Spirit (Acts 2:1–4). They were sanctified holy and wholly (Acts 15:8–9) and readied for the mammoth task of evangelizing the world. They went forth with boldness (4:31). As a result, their world was turned right side up!

After confessing and consecrating, we are ready to invite God to help us with constancy. Having been transformed into purity, we must focus on Christian maturity. Consecration is like achieving the legal status of adulthood at age twenty-one. Suddenly privileges and rights— rights that we have never known before—become ours. Constancy, on the other hand, resembles the necessary growth that must take place throughout our adult life, through the good times and the bad.

In essence, Christian constancy means increasing in love, enlarging our capacity for God's love. Paul highlights constancy in his First Letter to the Thessalonians, when he says, "May the Lord make your love increase and overflow for each other and for everyone else, just as ours does for you" (3:12).

Love must grow and grow and grow in our hearts. We must do more than settle for consistency. Instead, we must constantly grasp for ever more of God's love. This can only bring about increasing glory for the One who is the source of all love.

Three invitations, but one guest: love. It is necessary for our personal salvation, for it alone opens the floodgates of God's presence. What's more, love is the ticket that allows us to enter the arena of effective witnessing as full participants.

Who could possibly refuse the universal offer to become authentic recipients of love/excellence? Far brighter it is than any Olympic torch. Far more beautiful than the most intricate ancient Greek sculptures. Far more honorable than being a warrior in Alexander's victorious army.

And we can be engulfed in this glorious light of God's excellence without having to earn his favor (Eph. 2:8–9; Titus 3:5). Unlike the Greeks of old, who trembled for fear of Zeus' wrath for slight imperfections of conduct, we approach our God with confidence and trust (Heb. 4:16). We know all the while that he graciously offers to bestow his excellence to us as we will to do his will.

Biblical excellence is a glorious ideal for every Christian. It is a standard that activates our best energies and creativity, causing us to live our lives as he intended. Why? Because biblical excellence means divine love.

This is love observed in the excellencies of nature: brilliant tropical flowers in Hawaii, majestic geese in flight. This is love seen in excellent human expressions: Mother Teresa's sacrificial service, life-risking heroism at the site of a plane crash. But also it is love that makes us inwardly holy and at peace with the One who gives us ultimate fulfillment in our earthly existence—the One who promises us an inheritance in his eternal kingdom "that fadeth not away."

God is ready to assume full responsibility for the life wholly yielded to him. — Andrew Murray

Rather than giving God our ability, he wants our accessibility. — Earl G. Lee

Behold the turtle who makes progress only when he sticks his neck out. — Cecil Parker

5

Pursuing with Fervent Heart

The sound of some statements is like music to our ears. For example:

It's benign, not malignant.

All is forgiven.

It's a healthy baby.

The war is over!

We could all come up with our own list of statements that soothe our emotions, pour hope into our spirits, and bring deep comfort to our total beings.

But one statement should be near the top of all our lists: "Excellent job!" It means we have performed well. We have met, and even exceeded, the expectations of others— on a football field, in a classroom, or at the work place. We want our parents, employers, and peers to approve of our actions. When they assign the term *excellent* to what we've striven to do, we are pleased.

As followers of Christ, we yearn for his approval. We need to know that he considers us to be excellent, and to be doing things excellently, in our daily lives. Then, in that great day of judgment, we will hear him say the greatest words we will ever hear: "Well done, good and faithful servant! You have been faithful with a few things; I will put you in charge of many things. Come and share your master's happiness!" (Matt. 25:21).

But to know this fact is not enough. To realize that biblical excellence is divinely implanted *agapē* love will not suffice. To comprehend the ways in which we invite that love into our life is insufficient.

The simple fact is that to know is not necessarily to do. People know that traveling more than fifty-five miles per hour costs lives, that smoking causes cancer, that gossip injures innocent people. But, in each of these cases and in so many more, awareness has failed to bring about needed changes. In spite of education, intelligent Americans continue in self-destructive ways, consciously choosing to live foolishly and even flaunting their self-destructive behavior.

All of us have the problem of knowing more than we implement. We eat, drink, talk, work, play in excess. We neglect to write letters when we know we should, to fix a broken car, to rid ourselves of an arrogant attitude. We fail to follow through with putting what we know into practice.

We declare our reasons: "Not enough time." "Tried to improve before and failed." "It's not as bad as it seems." "Others get by, why not me?" "It's because of heredity." "God knows I'm human."

Don't misunderstand. Education is important. We need to become increasingly aware. To know that excellence/love is necessary and available is a crucial first step. But it is only a first step. In addition, we must be motivated to action. Paul instructs the Philippians to "work out [their] salvation with fear and trembling" (Phil. 2:12). Similarly, Hebrews assures us that God "rewards those who earnestly seek him" (11:6). There is a need to engage the will in discipline. We need to act on what we know.

To have authentic Christian excellence, we must gear ourselves to follow the biblical admonitions discussed in the last chapter. We must prepare for change. We must anticipate, in faith, that we will be increasingly allowing our lives to respond to his love. Our attitude must be one of expectant readiness.[1] Motivated to march forward!

But are all motives pure? Is it not possible to be motivated to attain biblical excellence but for the wrong reasons?

God's Gift for My Glory

Satan tricks us into thinking we can attain *agapē* love for our own benefit so the payoff package has our own name on it.

First, we're lured into believing that we are earning merit by our "bite-the-bullet" kind of obedience. As a result, we see ourselves as slaves, not sacraments. We submit to the yoke of painful duty in order to feel good about ourselves.

Second, Satan tempts us into the dangerous trap of legalism. This motivation finds ego satisfaction in doing what's necessary to be on God's list of very special people.

---

1. According to author Earl G. Lee, even spiritual "rest" is usually hard-earned. Hebrews states, "Let us labour therefore to enter into that rest" (4:11, KJV). Or, as the *Amplified Bible* admonishes, "Let us therefore be zealous and exert ourselves and strive diligently to enter into that rest [of God]." Once realized, this rest is not passive. It does not mean "being at ease." In Ps. 37:7, "rest" is taken from the Hebrew word that means "cease, be silent, submit in silence to what he ordains," in short, to be in a state of relaxed readiness to follow his guidance. Earl G. Lee, *The Cycle of Victorous Living* (Kansas City, Mo.: Beacon Hill, 1971), pp. 34—36.

The thought is: If I can be excellent/loving enough, he'll have to give me prominence in his kingdom. James and John, along with their conniving mother, had a problem with this (Mark 10:35–45).

Third, the enemy of our souls would have us become excellent in order to outshine those around us. How easy it is to root our motivation for excellence in competition so that our real goal is winning for our own glory.

Fourth, we can develop a lopsided view of excellence. Attempting to love excellently in one area of our lives, we can neglect other important areas. In my survey, author John White was right in saying that Christian excellence "is not so much a matter of being superior at some specific activity, as much as [it is] living an excellent, God-glorifying life."

Love must permeate all we do. Paul states, "So whether you eat or drink or whatever you do, do it all for the glory of God" (1 Cor. 10:31). A life of excellence penetrates and saturates every thought, attitude, and action so that, as the song declares, "Jesus [is] the Lord of all the kingdoms of [our] heart."

Finally, excellence must not be pursued because it leads to success. It is possible to choose Christian excellence over success, only to allow success to "come in the back door" of excellence. For example, we might love in order to gain others' affections or possessions. Such love has little resemblance to authentic *agapē* love.

Many of us evangelicals accept divine love, in becoming Christians, as the gateway to success. Assuring ourselves that we reject the world's gateway to the same goal, we fail to see (or admit) the inconsistency. This "God-as-sugarplum-fairy" mentality undercuts the entire existence of biblical excellence. With good reason Charles Colson refers to the "creeping greediness of the success gospel."[2]

2. Cynthia R. Schaible, "The Gospel of the Good Life," *Eternity*, February 1981, p. 21.

Cynthia R. Schaible in her insightful *Eternity* article spells out the inherent dangers in the gospel of success:

Excessively emphasizing the importance of a positive self-image, it ignores that we're worth little apart from Jesus (1 Cor. 2:2; Gal. 2:20).

The doctrine provides the tragic illusion that there is enough room at the "success peak" for everyone. It teaches that all believers with enough "name-it-and-claim-it" faith can become elite in this world.

Rather than emphasizing the dynamic, revolutionary changes that take place in the life of the Christian, through our Lord, proponents of this attitude focus on the superficial changes that only alter some behavior patterns, specifically the ones that are necessary to "get you ahead."

The doctrine inflates God's promises so that they are made to include more than our needs (Matt. 6:8, 32).

It deflates God's blessings. They are perceived as related only to material things (Luke 12:22–23).

The success gospel allows no room for God's sovereign will, failing to recognize that sometimes God blesses, but more often, his blessings seem to mysteriously surface through suffering (1 Peter 4:12–14).

This sensually appealing but counterfeit doctrine promotes an inevitable lack of sensitivity to responsible stewardship and with it a denouncement of authentic servanthood.[3]

As Christians, we must realize that our excellence results in a far more valuable treasure than temporal success. In fact, our greatest glory comes when, in the face of severe tribulation, we can clutch the "torch of divine love"

3. Ibid, pp. 21–23, 26–27.

tighter. We realize that our full reward will come later (John 14:2–3).

Having examined counterfeit motivations for pursuing Christian excellence, we once again remind ourselves of their fatal flaw: focusing attention on our own glory and profit.

Performing benevolent deeds is not enough. We can "speak in tongues of men and of angels," "prophe[sy]," "move mountains" (of difficulty), "give all [we] possess" and "surrender [our] bod[ies] to the flames" for the benefit of people (1 Cor. 13:1–3). But, in going to such extremes, we must determine whether we're doing such noble deeds for God's glory or for our own.

What is the best motive for attaining excellence in our life as a Christian? Put simply, it is seeking to glorify God.

Excellence Generated by an Altruistic Motive

Recall the last few words of the Lord's Prayer: "for Thine is the kingdom, and the power, and the glory forever. Amen." Truer words were never spoken. Our heavenly Father deserves all the glory—and forever. It follows that all biblical excellence that we attain to, which is his gift in the first place, must be returned to him. In this way he is glorified and honored and we have realized our chief purpose in life.

Author Jerry Bridges summarizes this point well: "Christian excellence is the quality of life that results when a Christian seeks to live out every area of his life with the aim of pleasing . . . and glorifying God. He is worthy of our most diligent efforts."

You may wonder: Doesn't Bridges have us reasonably comfortable, secure, and free Americans in mind? Glorifying God is our natural response for his blessings. But what about those who are harshly persecuted for their faith?

In his first epistle, Peter addressed such an audience in

the early church. These people lived in constant fear of oppression. The disciple Jesus called "the Rock" admonished them to be steadfast and to even rejoice in the midst of their trials, to be excellent in love in spite of all so that their faith would "glorify" God (1 Peter 2:12; 4:11, 16).

The motivation to glorify our Maker and his Son must be universal. As nature brings such glory to its Creator in so many beautiful and different ways, so we must attain Christian excellence for that same reason, in spite of our unique surroundings. Excellence for the glory of God!

If this is our motivation, we will humbly and gratefully accept his timeless and trustworthy ways of teaching us about his excellence. These ways likewise bring glory to his name.

God's Lesson Plans

First, we learn from God's written Word. As we learned in chapter 4, our Bible confronts us with the importance of Christian excellence.

The apostle Paul, standard-bearer and embodiment of such excellence, admonishes, "I want you to be able always to recognize the highest and the best, and to live sincere and blameless lives until the day of Jesus Christ" (Phil. 1:10, *Phillips*). Another version states, "That ye may approve things that are excellent" (KJV).

John Stapert, editor of the *Church Herald*, offered a helpful explanation of this verse in his response to the survey. The Greek word for "what is excellent" means "the things that differ." In short, as Christians, we must discern (v. 9) things that differ from being merely good. Ours must always be the highest and best. In another place, Paul instructed the Corinthian church to "covet earnestly the best gifts" (1 Cor. 12:31, KJV). In regard to the Greek word for "approve," Stapert suggested that it implies an investment of our total being rather than simply an intellectual consent.

This is an emphatic choice of words: "highest," "best," "approve," "a more excellent way." Such words are straightforward, direct, penetrating, and demanding, but necessary for our life to bring glory to God.

Second, God would have us learn from his incarnate Word, Jesus Christ. Christ is our model, our example, our incarnation for love-based excellence. Because of this, as Robert Murray McCheyne says, "For every [one] look at [ourselves, we should] take ten of Jesus Christ."

God's written lesson, as clear and helpful as it is, could not suffice. Our world needed a perfect embodiment of God's love. Our Lord is that embodiment. Because of him we have hope. The early church realized this. As E. Stanley Jones said, they "did not say in dismay: 'Look what the world has come to,' but, in delight, 'Look what has come into the world!' " Today we share that same hope.

In our day it is easy to lose sight of the real Jesus and to picture a synthetic, counterfeit Lord who neatly conforms to our hedonistic cravings. Edward Kuhlman put it well:

> Many speak of Jesus as if he were a character in a flat one-dimensional soap opera. Jesus comes with manicured nails and razorcut coiffure. He comes as one of the Osmonds with teeth straight, white, and free of cavities. He comes as an Emmy winner with chest hair showing through the open shirt front, a gold chain encircling his tanned throat. Of course, he's wearing Jordache jeans.

This is not the kind of excellence he possessed. Rather, Jesus was the supreme combatant of satanic power, described in Hebrews as the One who "learned obedience from what he suffered" (5:8), the "author and perfecter of our faith, who for the joy set before him endured the cross, scorning its shame" (12:2). We are invited to "consider him who endured such opposition from sinful men, so that [we] will not grow weary and lose heart" (12:3).

He was, by no means, a softy. Instead, he was engaged in a constant and agonizing fight against the powerful forces of evil. But through it all he remained excellent, loving the "unlovable."

Unlike others considered great in history, he provided a living example. He is more than a reference point in the past—One who taught valuable insights; one who exemplified what he taught. Our Savior died for our sins, the just for the unjust, so that we might be reconciled to God in our lifetime. But even more than this, he rose again to saturate us with his presence every moment (Gal 2:20)—to take the place of what we are. As W. Ian Thomas put it, "His *strength* for our *weakness*! His *wisdom* for our *folly*! His *drive* for our *drift*! His *grace* for our *greed*! His *love* for our *lust*! His *peace* for our *problems*! His *plenty* for our *poverty*!" A living example.

So this is Christian excellence: divinely implanted *agapē* love, undergirded by the right motive—the desire to bring glory to God. It is taught to us through the lessons he has provided: his written and incarnate Words.

But you may ask: What happens to the Christian excellence that is motivated by a desire to please him? Does God receive, and keep, all the glory for himself? Or are others blessed?

The Results of Excellence

In a word, God's glory continually recycles and recirculates, expanding all the while. Although our heavenly Father deserves, and greatly appreciates, all the glory we send his way, we become the major beneficiaries. Those of us who lose ourselves (selflessly honor him) find ourselves blessed beyond measure (John 12:25). And it happens because we refuse to be excellent for that reason!

First, our world benefits when we glorify God through our excellence. Others are shown an example of the fulfilled life as the Father intends it to be lived. Our influence takes on a ripple effect as it impacts those who desperately need a reason to exist.

Technology has inundated our planet with gadgets and conveniences. As someone declared, it has made dentistry painless, bicycles chainless, carriages horseless, laws enforceless, cooking fireless, telegraphy wireless, coffee caffeineless, births weanless, oranges seedless, putting greens weedless, roads dustless, steel rustless, tennis courts sodless—and, in so doing, our lives godless.

Our world needs people who excel in reflecting God's love more than it needs advanced technology. The Bible refers to such persons as the "aroma of Christ among those who are being saved and those who are perishing" (2 Cor. 2:15). A few verses later, they are termed a "letter from Christ" written "with the Spirit of the living God . . . on tablets of human hearts" (3:3). Ephesians 2:10 likens us to "God's workmanship" or masterpiece that he exhibits to reflect his own excellence in a sin-sick world!

My survey posed the question: Why is Christian excellence so desperately needed in our world today?

Television has debilitated moral standards and reduced time spent in [reflecting on God]—Kenneth Taylor

We have an incredible ethical crisis which threatens the disintegration of our world at an ever-accelerating rate.—Paul T. Culbertson

American society has gradually moved farther . . . away from its Christian heritage. Consequently . . . Christian values are being replaced by [those that are] humanistic.—Virginia Patterson

Because the world is suffering greatly from irresponsibility, mediocrity, and distorted values.—Howard A. White

All of these responses convey truth. Christian excellence is needed today. It has always been needed, but especially today when we have power to destroy our planet in minutes, when two-thirds of the people who have ever lived are presently living, when more than one billion are starving to death (ten thousand each day).

But what is even more crucial, there are more opportunities for Christian witness than ever before! Wade Coggins, executive director of Evangelical Foreign Missions, Associaton, spoke the truth: "We must demonstrate through Christian excellence that the gospel transforms and gives a new way of life. If our words are not backed up by such excellence we will lose the attention of the world, and fail to bring them to Christ."

Second, we as Christians reap bountifully when we glorify God through loving excellence. Not only is there a ripple effect, but also there is a boomerang effect. Paul declares, "And we, who with unveiled faces all reflect the Lord's glory, are being transformed into his likeness with ever-increasing glory, which comes from the Lord ..." (2 Cor. 3:18).

We are not glorifying ourselves nor glorifying God in order to bring glory to ourselves. Rather, we are glorifying God! Then, as an unanticipated effect, we are increasingly showered with his blessing and glory. This is like a surprise package presented to the loving Christian. But, when you really think about it, it is not so surprising after all. Our God always gives—and returns what we offer to him tenfold, a hundredfold!

Two Gifts in One

God increases our supply of excellence in two ways. We increase in Christian excellence. Perceiving our life to be a Christian vocation, we strive to develop our talents and maximize our strengths, becoming "a workman who does not need to be ashamed" (2 Tim. 2:15). But our excellence is Christian because we are motivated by the principle of love. We know that this brings glory to the excellent One.

In addition to receiving more Christian excellence, we

progressively become a more excellent Christian. After confession and consecration (see chap. 4), we focus our attention on constancy. Having received the gift of purity, we commit ourselves to maturity. Ephesians 4:15 encapsulates this principle: "We will in all things grow up into him who is the Head, that is, Christ." Similarly, Peter instructs, "But grow in the grace and knowledge of our Lord and Savior Jesus Christ" (2 Peter 3:18).

This second kind of excellence has to do with refining our Christian walk, enlarging our capacity for love, and allowing that love to permeate all we do, say, and are.

This can and will take place as we "walk in the light, as he is in the light" (1 John 1:7). This same verse goes on to promise us that "the blood of Jesus, his Son, purifies [i.e., keeps on purifying] us from every sin." God's spiritual filter system remains intact and operates to stop evil from dominating our life. In addition, that system expands in its capacity to generate *agapē* love. The result is more glory for God—and a return of that glory to our world and life.

A Plan for Refurbishing

Renovation implies complete renewal from the ground up, but refurbishing means improvement of what exists. To refurbish our house is to do such things as paint the outside, redo the landscaping, and add new shutters.

After being born again and sanctified wholly (spiritual renovation) we must adopt a plan for continual growth in Christian love (spiritual refurbishing). As is true of repairing a house, results cannot be expected overnight. Progressive excellence in our Christian life will be just that, progressive. In fact, it is likely to seem regressive at times— taking a three-steps-forward-and-one-backward pattern. But it is the direction in which we are heading that is crucial.

In part 3, a plan for continual refurbishing is presented.

Each chapter presents a standard of excellence, based on God's Word, that will increase our capacity for (and refine our expression of) *agapē* love. We need to apply each standard in ways that relate to our own life, but apply them nevertheless. The Holy Spirit will guide us as we do this, for he is our Counselor (John 14:16–17).

May our love-commitment deepen. May our giving glory to God increase. May our witness to a lost world become progressively effective. And may we be open to making the needed midcourse corrections so that we may become more like what he would have us become.

Psalm 36:7 declares, "How excellent is thy loving kindness, O God!" (KJV). To comprehend this declaration fully is to desire this excellent, steadfast, divine love for ourselves—above everything! May that deep desire translate into a humble willingness to consider prayerfully his direction as we examine the principles of spiritual growth.

Part **3**

Excellence
Nurtured in Our Walk

It was not the outer grandeur of the Roman but the inner simplicity of the Christian that lived on through the ages. — Charles Lindbergh

God does not comfort us only to make us comfortable – rather He does it to make us comforters. — Navigator's *Daily Walk Bible*

If it is more blessed to give than to receive, then most of us are content to let the other fellow have the greater blessing. — Shailer Mathews

6

The Towel and the Cross

My friend and I were talking about what it means to be a true servant of Jesus Christ. He began to tell me a story. It centered around his father, who took pride in his skill at playing checkers. Not content to merely win, he gleefully pulverized his opponents. They were beaten, then ridiculed until they were demolished in spirit.

Family members and neighbors intensely disliked playing checkers with my friend's father. They considered it humiliating. Why should his insatiable ego be fed at their expense? They had a point.

But there was one who did fine playing this Muhammad Ali of checkers. Who was it? My friend's mother. How did she survive his onslaught and arrogance? It was simple. While his goal was winning, hers was getting the game over as soon as possible. So her strategy was to give away her checkers quickly. An average game took seconds. His craving was satisfied—he won. But she was also delighted. Her giving had made him happy.

Our world is full of takers. Most live according to the strategy of my friend's father—winning, rubbing it in, thriving on competition while victories keep coming. Losing, or even having to share in victory, is considered unacceptable. Such persons live by the philosophy of the late football coach Vince Lombardi, who declared, "Winning . . . is the only thing!"

God offers us a contrasting standard. His idea is more like that of my friend's mother. He gave away all he had so that we might reap the benefits. And he keeps on giving to each of us every day. His was (and is) the excellence of unparalleled generosity. And so will be ours—if we grow in his kind of excellence.

One word captures his brand of spontaneous, sacrificial giving. What is it? Servanthood.

It's in the Book

God's Word repeatedly showcases the idea of servanthood. The most common term for "servant" is *doulos*, which means "slave."[1] Ironically, the ancient world considered it to be a title of humiliation. People frowned upon the idea of being subservient, of putting a master's interests before their own.

By contrast, the Bible describes the greatest of biblical personalities as servants. Moses the supreme lawgiver (Deut. 34:5), Joshua the victorious commander (Josh.

---

1. 1 Cor. 4:1. In this passage Paul employs another term for "servant": *hupēretēs*. According to William Barclay, the term originally meant "a rower on the lower bank of a trireme, one of the slaves who pulled at the great sweeps which moved the triremes through the sea." It was pointed out that some commentators use this as a picture of Christ the pilot, who directs the course of the ship, and Paul as the servant accepting the orders of his Pilot, laboring only as his Master directs. William Barclay, *The Daily Study Bible: Letters to the Corinthians* (Philadelphia: Westminster, 1955), p. 40.

24:29), David the greatest of Israel's kings (Ps. 78:70), and the prophets (Isa. 20:3; Amos 3:7) were described as the servants of God. In the New Testament, James (1:1), Jude (1), Paul (Rom. 1:1), and Peter (2 Peter 1:1) proudly claim the same title.

The idea of "servant" fits well with that of "lord" (*kurios*), meaning "absolute owner of a person or thing." *Kurios* was Paul's favorite title for Jesus, his Lord and Master. He realized that Jesus had lovingly died for his salvation. As a result, he no longer belonged to himself. He had been "bought at a price" (1 Cor. 7:23). As Christ's slave, he became his master's herald (message-bearer), apostle (envoy or ambassador), and teacher (interpreter) (2 Tim. 1:11).

In addition, the New Testament uses the title *servant of Christ* for all Christians. "He who was a free man when he was called is Christ's slave" (1 Cor. 7:22b). Again, in Ephesians 6:6b, the apostle instructs us to live "like slaves of Christ, doing the will of God from [our] heart[s]."

But what, specifically, does it mean to grow in servanthood? William Barclay offers light. For him, growth in servanthood means becoming

inalienably possessed by God

unqualifiedly at the disposal of God

unquestionably obedient to God

constantly in the service of God[2]

Ownership, availability, obedience, and service. That's what it means to grow toward this crucial biblical ideal.

Greatness Redefined

As they trekked along the dusty road, James and John realized that the end was near. Jesus was on his way to

2. Ibid., *The Letters of James and Peter*, pp. 345–46.

Jerusalem for the final time. He had explained to them all that was to happen.

With the urging of their ambitious mother, the brothers decided to ask for positions of special prominence in Christ's kingdom. These were not simply positions of prominence; rather, they were *the* positions of prominence right next to their Lord.

To his conniving disciples, Jesus announced a new standard of greatness:

> You know that those who are regarded as rulers of the Gentiles lord it over them, and their high officials exercise authority over them. Not so with you. Instead, whoever wants to become great among you must be your servant, and whoever wants to be first must be slave of all. [Mark 10:42–44]

Slave of all! Not vice presidents, but street sweepers, toilet cleaners, garbage men, people who are content with, and even grateful for, the dirty work. What a stinging rebuke to James and John, who had mistakenly assumed that Christ's kingdom is one of earthly pomp and splendor, and greatness consists of place and position (i.e., success).

In essence, Jesus taught them (and us) that this world's idea of worth cannot be carried over into his spiritual realm. In Christ's kingdom, there is a complete reversal of earth's values. In heaven, gold is used to pave roads. His lesson: Not the number of one's servants, but the number whom one serves, is the heavenly criterion for greatness. The final reward will be commensurate with the greatness of service humbly rendered.

Of course, Christ's own earthly ministry exemplified this principle: "For even the Son of Man did not come to be served, but to serve, and to give his life as a ransom for many." Again, in Luke 22:27 we read, "But I am among you as one who serves."

In serving, Christ became our supreme example. We are called upon to follow in his footsteps of servanthood. As someone said, he became what we are (man) to make us what he is (servant). That was why he picked up the towel (John 13:4) and soon thereafter the cross (Luke 23:25). Now it's our turn. For, as he declares in Matthew 10:24–25, "A student is not above his teacher, nor a servant above his master. It is enough for the student to be like his teacher, and the servant like his master."

Becoming his servant, and later sharing in his glory, sounds so inviting. What an honor to identify with our Lord and Master. If he considers servanthood essential, how can we settle for anything less!

Unfortunately, often our best intentions are not sufficient. We encounter unforeseen difficulties that make servanthood little more than an elusive dream. What are some of these?

Satan's Spoilers

The famous conductor Leonard Bernstein was once asked, "What is the most difficult instrument to play?" Without hesitation he replied, "Second fiddle." Then he explained, "I can get plenty of first violinists, but to find one who plays *second* violin with as much enthusiasm or *second* French horn or *second* flute, now that's a problem. And yet if no one plays second, we have no harmony."[3]

Many Christians shy away from servanthood because, in reality, it means playing second fiddle, taking a back seat, going to the end of the line, relinquishing the credit, doing things in secret so that there's no fanfare. The world advocates the opposite: toot your own horn, push ahead to the front of the line, demand credit, showcase all contributions.

3. Charles R. Swindoll, *Improving Your Serve: The Art of Unselfish Living* (Waco: Word, 1981), p. 34.

Although sacrificing isn't difficult for me, sacrificing in secret is. That's probably why I give others a bad time about it.

Not long ago my mother heard a medical missonary tell about having to use razor blades instead of scalpels. Imagine a poor African lying on an operating table with the doctor cutting around his vital parts with razor blades. The very thought makes my skin crawl. Well, the heartstrings of my mom were plucked. She contributed a sum of money to purchase the scalpels.

But it wasn't long before my philanthropist mother began telling me about all the positive reactions of others. Many people were giving her "strokes" for giving the money. Among themselves they were saying, "Did you hear? Mrs. Johnston gave a sizable sum to the missionary—even though she's on a fixed income." And Mom was savoring every delicious compliment.

"Mom," I said, "don't you know that your sacrificial gift is scoreless with God?" She asked, "Why do you say that?" "Because you've bragged to everyone. The Bible says that if we get the credit in this life, we certainly won't score points in heaven."

She looked at me with a big grin and said, "I've given quite a bit in secret in the past. This time around I wanted to enjoy some of the reward in this life!" An honest answer to my teasing question.

But don't we all find it difficult to fade into the background after being benevolent? The "no-strings-attached" gift suddenly has plenty of strings, cords, and even ropes attached. What began as a secret, loving act of benevolence ends up being proclaimed from the rooftops (or in a testimony at church). Bernstein was right. It cuts against the grain of our nature to play second fiddle!

Second, while it's hard to play second fiddle, we find that it is easy to fake servanthood. Frauds are everywhere. Some obtain mail-order "doctorates" for twenty-five dollars. Others offer us "the deal of our lives"—which turns out to be swampland in Florida or a car that formerly belonged to someone like Evel Knievel. In fact, I know a person who parks in the "handicap zone" and limps all the way into the store!

Some fakes are humorous. But one kind isn't funny at all. In fact, this pretender is pathetic. It is the person who feigns being a servant of Jesus Christ.

Such an individual is being deceptive at the expense of God's kingdom, much like a communist spy who claims allegiance to the "stars and stripes." He claims to represent something that, in reality, he strongly opposes while still receiving all the benefits.

Faking servanthood isn't difficult:

Give to big-name projects—favorites of those in power.

Advertise your generosity indirectly with exaggeration.

Develop the "look" of piety and sincerity.

Perform unimportant tasks—the jobs nobody wants— but in front of the "right" people.

These and other measures will gain the attention of God's gullible people. For, as his Word proclaims, "Man looks at the outward appearance . . ." (1 Sam. 16:7). Christians, wanting to think the best about others, are especially vulnerable to being deceived in this way.

Realizing the vulnerability of God's community of believers, and seeing the rich payoff for being perceived as a servant, scores resort to carrying off the charade of servanthood. They go through the motions, use the right words, and look the right ways at the right times. And people are fooled.

Third, some people are content to play second fiddle, and even do it without the slightest trace of deceit, but in being a servant everything seems to backfire. Sometimes authentic servanthood isn't perceived as such. Instead, it is suspected, criticized, and even ridiculed. People ask,

"Who's he trying to impress?" One survey respondent rightly declared, "We [often] see pacesetters as trouble-makers [who show us up] by comparison." People who set the pace with sacrifice are resented the most because they produce guilt in those who realize their own shortcomings.

Then there are well-intentioned servants who use the wrong methods. They are enthusiastic, courageous, sincere, but a bit impulsive and unwise.

Peter was such a person. It was the week before the crucifixion. He boldly proclaimed to our Lord that he would never forsake him (Matt. 26:33). Soon thereafter, this "Rock" walked with Jesus to Gethsemane. In a rapid succession of events, the man of many promises twice went to sleep while Jesus prayed; cut off a soldier's ear when he reached out to seize the Savior; three times denied that he was a follower of (or even knew) the Master; wept bitterly (Matt. 26:75) at his failures.

Peter, I know you better than you think. I've risen from my knees after a time of close communion and inspiration, intending to be completely servantlike in everything that was to happen that day. But then, when the real test came, I brought only disappointment to the God I serve. Inwardly I could only weep bitterly.

Pressures—the flat tire, the undeserved insult, the hard, efficient work that goes unrecognized—have a way of spoiling our plans. All of a sudden attitudes emerge that choke the Spirit of Christ. Like Peter, we go to sleep (retreat from responsibility), cut off some poor man's ear (become aggressive), deny our Lord (seize control of our lives), and end up demolished in spirit.

But is such a chain of events inevitable? Are we destined to failure? Is true New Testament servanthood beyond our reach? Not at all. We can look around and see persons who become better servants with every passing day. They warm our hearts and give us hope.

What seem to be the characteristics of such persons?

By examining this question, perhaps we can obtain some needed direction of our own lives.

Applying the Formula of Servanthood

Most people can probably agree with much that has been said in this chapter. The need for attaining love/excellence in our servanthood is evident. And, yes, there are definite barriers along the way.

But what about becoming more servantlike with each passing day? Are there fundamentals that must be mastered? If so, what are they?

First, we must be prepared to accept inconvenient interruptions and to accept them as providential gifts from God. How often we squeeze God and his work into our busy schedule. As an inevitable result, he is shortchanged and so are we. There's the five-minute "good-morning—goodby" time in the morning, the "wait-'til-nobody's-looking" blitz prayer at mealtime, the "sorry-I'm-too-busy" response to a request for service.

When we are true slaves of our heavenly Father, his timing will be our timing—even if it means losing track of time. Jesus often did. Neither he nor anyone else wondered about time when he was astounding the scholars in the temple at age twelve. And how about the time that he taught on the mountain? Everyone's attention remained riveted on him, even though their stomachs were growling with hunger. They became so hungry that he had to perform a miracle!

Desiring to be more servantlike, we must increasingly involve our best energies in worshiping him and helping his children in need, when they are in need. Have you noticed? Needs and crises refuse to conform to our schedules. In fact, they seem to sabotage our schedules. Consider our Lord's parable of the Good Samaritan. This fellow was severely inconvenienced. His schedule was torn to shreds. His travel money was handed over to a strange hotel manager for someone he didn't even know. Yet he was not deprived of the joy of being inconvenienced for God.

You may think that in those times, people didn't have all that much to do. How about today? Are there really any busy persons who drop everything to care for someone in need? Do you know of any? I do.

He doesn't know I know. In fact, that was the whole idea. He didn't want anyone to know. He is a presiding officer in the denomination to which I belong. If anyone has a more demanding schedule, I don't know who it is.

It was the big day of dedication for a beautiful new church building in Dallas. The crowd gathered. There was only one problem. The speaker was uncharacteristically late. What had happened? People began to worry. Some even panicked, which is not unlike church people on such occasions.

The speaker arrived in time to perform his duties and apologized for being tardy. The service ended. Everyone went home.

It wasn't until the next week that the church learned the real story. A woman called the church office. Her story was beautiful. She had experienced severe car trouble on the busiest freeway in Dallas. Cars raced by. After what seemed like an eternity, one car stopped and backed up to where she was standing.

She was at wit's end, exhausted, disgusted, even angry. The tall stranger spoke calm words of comfort. Then he took her to get assistance at a time when most everything was closed. Finally, help was located. Her car was repaired. And the Good Samaritan disappeared. She called the church to express gratitude.

Inconvenienced? Certainly he was, and ever concerned about his obligation to the church. But that didn't keep him from stopping. We too must be willing to interrupt our schedules to assist someone in need. This is the first principle of servanthood. But how do we know when someone is in need?

Second, increased servanthood means increased spiritual sensitivity to (and awareness of) others. This means turning away from ourselves and toward others. It means having invisible radar that is constantly scanning to locate those who are hurting, those for whom our Master deeply cares.

Most of us are absorbed by thoughts of personal well-being. Every situation, circumstance, person, and object is judged according to how it will better or worsen our life. No wonder we use personal pronouns so often. We constantly bore others with inconsequential trivia about our own existence.

I worked in a bottle factory to put myself through college. It amazed me how my fellow workers used one another as listening boards. There was rarely give-and-take communication. Rather it was: "You're my captive audience. Now you listen to what is important in my life. I demand it."

To cite an example, I overheard two women talking. One took out a miniature picture album and made the other listen to every detail of her family history. But the other woman didn't remain passive. She would break in whenever her friend took a breath. She told about *her* family—never referring to anything that had been said concerning the other family. Neither listened to the other.

As servants of Jesus Christ, we must break out of our self-orbits. Our job, possessions, security, family must become secondary. "And we ought to lay down our lives for our brothers" (1 John 3:16b). I do not take this to mean martyrdom, although it could also refer to that. Rather, it seems as though the reference is to committing our lives to the lives of others, especially those who are in need. Verse 17 goes on to say, "If anyone has material possessions and sees his brother in need but has no pity on him, how can the love of God be in him?"

Satan distracts us from bearing the burdens of others. A hardening effect sets in. We're used to seeing people killed on television. We drive through delapidated ghettos without the slightest sense of compassion. Then, when another shares an earnest, desperate need we yawn and say to ourselves, "You've got your problems and I've got mine."

God wants to sensitize us to the hurt he feels when he sees human suffering. Being his servant means accepting his heartbreak, deeply caring for others' pain and suffering, and doing something about it.

Finally, becoming more servantlike means looking to God alone for reward. We should not anticipate the applause of the ones we have helped—be they strangers, friends, or even family members!

Servanthood is so special because it is done for God and is rewarded by God. In Christ's Sermon on the Mount, he explains that our heavenly Father sees our piety, giving, and prayers done in secrecy. Then he responds by rewarding us openly (Matt. 6:1–6, KJV).

One thing has always been hard for me to understand. After accepting inconvenience, becoming sensitive to another's need, and even responding sacrificially to that need, I've noticed that the persons helped often seem to resent me thereafter. Perhaps the recipient of my benevolence feels embarrassed that he needed assistance. Our society praises self-sufficiency and condemns dependency. Or maybe he fears that I'll feel that he owes me a debt of gratitude and I'll expect payment. All I know is that often a barrier arises between me and the person I've assisted, even when it has been a "let's-never-talk-about-it-again" situation.

But when this occurs, I remind myself that helping is a spontaneous act, as natural as breathing, for his servants. Its focus must be on bringing glory to his name. Finally, in addition to rewarding us later in heaven, he never fails to reward our inner spirit. We are given a deep inner peace and assurance and an abiding sense of his approval—the greatest gift of all!

Silent, Secret Service

Will we become increasingly servantlike? We must! Will it be rewarding? Immensely! For servanthood is a giant step toward Christian excellence.

Ruth Harms Calkin has written a poem entitled "I Wonder." Desiring to follow our Lord's example, we will answer yes to its closing question!

>You know, Lord, how I serve You
>With great emotional fervor
>In the limelight.
>You know how eagerly I speak for You
>At a women's club.
>You know how I effervesce when I promote
>A fellowship group.
>You know my genuine enthusiasm
>At a Bible study.
>
>But how would I react, I wonder
>If You pointed to a basin of water
>And asked me to wash the calloused feet
>Of a bent and wrinkled old woman
>Day after day
>Month after month
>In a room where nobody saw
>And nobody knew.

The older I grow the more clearly I perceive the dignity and winning beauty of simplicity in thought, conduct, and speech: a desire to simplify all that is complicated and to treat everything with the greatest of naturalness and clarity. —Pope John XXIII

The gospel can be condensed into these simple words: "Jesus loves me this I know, for the Bible tells me so." —Karl Barth

This world has enough for everyone's need, but not enough for everyone's greed. —Mahatma Gandhi

Civilization is a limitless multiplication of unnecessary necessities. —Mark Twain

7

Lowly, But Not Losers

FIGURE 1

To Queue If All Lines Are Busy
- You Will Hear a Callback Announcement
- Depress 5
- System Will Announce a Three-Digit Queue Number
- Hang Up Handset
- You Will Receive Three Short Rings When a Line Is Available
- Lift Handset
- System Will Repeat Three-Digit Queue Number
- Call Is Placed

The instructions in Figure 1 are not those for launching a rocket from Cape Canaveral. They come from an instruction sheet on my desk.

At the university where I teach, we recently installed a four-million-dollar, computerized, twenty-first-century IBX telephone system. It does everything but boil water and scratch your back. It has enough complicated options to give Ma Bell a migraine headache.

To name a few, you can place and retrieve a call on hold while entertaining the waiting party with recorded music; set up a seven-way conference; program into the computer for automatic dialing; leave an electronic message if there is no answer; or add parties to an existing call.

There's only one problem. The system is so complex that, in spite of an extensive seminar, few people have learned to use it effectively. When it is used incorrectly, the result is frustration: eardrum-splitting static and whistles or reprimands from the annoyed who receive repeated "wrong number" calls. People are able to read the names of the "intruders" on the digital screen. I sometimes long for the simplicity of the old-fashioned, two-party crank phone. I'm sure it would make *me* less cranky!

We all have areas of our lives that we want to simplify. There are the "self-cleaning" ovens that won't, the "maintenance-free" car batteries that aren't, and the "it-does-it-by-itself" lawnmower that doesn't. To repair them requires the knowledge of a mechanical engineer. And how about those new, revolutionary filing systems which permanently lose valuable papers? It takes a photographic memory to remember the subject categories!

But this relates to things. What about relationships with people? Ask a Pentagon employee about the staggering complexity of that operation. Or, volunteer to serve on a committee. (Someone defined a committee as the unable, appointed by the unwilling, to do the unnecessary.)

Better yet, carefully listen to the sermon of a minister who tries to impress with his vocabulary. You're apt to hear words that make you dizzy—like "supralapsarianism" and "premillennialism." (One exasperated layman was overheard declaring, "Six days a week our pastor is invisible; then, on the seventh, he's unintelligible!")

We need simplicity in all areas of life, especially our Christian walk. The Bible calls us back to God's basics, inviting us to discover (or rediscover) those simple essentials that can give our lives abundant meaning and maximum fulfillment. Let's carefully examine its timeless and valuable message.

The Bible: Advocate of Simplicity

Our world honors success, temporal security, and status—goals that often complicate life. Furthermore, "experts" can't seem to agree on the means of attaining these goals. As someone remarked, "If you lined up all the world's experts, end to end, they'd never reach a conclusion."

Biblical writers, on the other hand, spotlight simplicity. The psalmist explains that the simple are revived and made wise by God's law (19:7). Also, they freely receive his generous protection (116:6). Paul instructs the Romans (12:8, KJV) to give with simplicity. To the church at Corinth he states that he has dealt with it "in simplicity and godly sincerity, not with fleshly wisdom, but by the grace of God" (2 Cor. 1:12, KJV).[1] Finally, he expresses fear that Satan might deceive its members, "so [their] minds [will] be corrupted from the simplicity that is in Christ" (2 Cor. 11:3, KJV).[2]

But what exactly does God's Word mean when it refers to being simple? What key themes emerge from this important concept?

1. *Phillips* translation of 2 Cor. 1:12: "Our dealings with you, ... have been absolutely aboveboard and sincere before God. They have not been marked by any wordly wisdom, but by the grace of God."
2. *Phillips* translation of 2 Cor. 11:3: "I am afraid that your minds may be seduced from a singlehearted devotion to him by the same subtle means that the serpent used toward Eve."

First, God chooses the weak and lowly rather than those who connive to gain power. Lowly persons are described in Christ's Beatitudes—the "poor in spirit," "those who mourn," "the meek," "those who hunger and thirst for righteousness," "the merciful," "pure in heart," "peacemakers," and "those who are persecuted because of righteousness" (Matt. 5:3–10).

Paul informed the Corinthians that they weren't nearly as great as they thought. In addition, he said that for his most crucial assignments God often uses people thought to be insignificant. In the apostle's words, "God chose the foolish things of the world to shame the wise . . . the weak things . . . to shame the strong . . . the lowly . . . and the despised things . . . so that no one may boast before him" (1 Cor. 1:27–29).

We are inclined to think God chooses "big names" to do important jobs. So we showcase celebrities who are Christians: baseball stars, politicians, beauty queens, millionaires. The Corinthians thought the same way. But Paul disagreed. He knew that our heavenly Father uses little people. His key point: It's our weakness God wants, more than our strength; our accessibility, more than our ability.

But didn't Paul have impressive credentials? Not really. He admits to not being much of a preacher—"preach[ing] the gospel—not with words of human wisdom, lest the cross of Christ be emptied of its power" (1 Cor. 1:17).

Paul's critics went even further, saying that "in person he is unimpressive and his speaking amounts to nothing" (2 Cor. 10:10). The *Acts of Paul and Thecla* (a third-century apocryphal writing) describes his appearance: "low stature, bald, crooked thighs, handsome legs, hollow eyed . . . with a crooked nose."[3]

In addition, Paul had a serious defect which he described as a "thorn in the flesh" and which God refused

3. William Stewart McBirnie, *The Search for the Twelve Apostles* (Wheaton: Tyndale House, 1982), p. 291.

to take away. In the words of his divine Master, "My power is made perfect in weakness" (2 Cor. 12:9). Paul's weakness allowed God's power to flow through him better, so that he could proclaim, "For when I am weak, then I am strong" (2 Cor. 12:10).

Paul didn't boast of his graduate degrees, but of his weakness: poverty, beatings, stoning, shipwrecks, imprisonments. He declared, "If I must boast, I will boast of the things that show my weakness" (2 Cor. 11:30).[4]

What is true concerning Paul is true about so many others in God's Word. Old Testament leaders were weakness personified! When God asked Moses to lead the children of Israel he claimed that he wasn't good enough (Exod. 3:11), lacked credibility (4:1), and lacked eloquence (4:10). Others who were chosen by God responded initially in a similar manner:

Gideon: "My clan is the weakest in Manasseh, and I am the least in my family" (Judg. 6:15).

Saul: "But am I not a Benjamite, from the smallest tribe of Israel, and is not my clan the least of all the clans of the tribe of Benjamin?" (1 Sam. 9:21).

David: "Who am I, and what is my family or my father's clan in Israel . . . ?" (1 Sam. 18:18). "I'm only a poor man and little known" (18:23). "Whom are you pursuing? A dead dog? A flea?" (24:14).

Solomon: "But I am only a little child and do not know how to carry out my duties" (1 Kings 3:7).

Amos: "I was neither a prophet nor a prophet's son, but I was a shepherd, and I also took care of sycamore-fig trees" (Amos 7:14).

Gayle D. Erwin graphically describes our Lord's disciples, whom he terms "a motley crew":

4. John F. Alexander, "Weakness: An Entryway for God," *Other Side,* September 1983, pp. 8–9.

[Jesus] went to the streets and wharves and picked out the strangest crew ever to be sent out on a mission to change the world. Had you been walking within fifty feet of them you probably would have detected the odor of fish.

He had a Zealot and a tax collector on the team which is a combination not unlike a Black revolutionary and a Ku Klux Klan member. Some of them had heavily identifiable accents inappropriate to the need for eloquence on the team. He was found constantly among the sordid—from the violent to the crafty to the sensual.[5]

God chose (and still chooses) those convinced of their own dependency on him to confound the proud and powerful; the weak of the world to confound the wise. He inspired his prophet, Ezekiel, to declare, "All the trees of the field will know that I the LORD bring down the tall tree and make the low tree grow tall" (Ezek. 17:24). Truly, it is the "meek" (the humble; those who manifest a lowly spirit) who will inherit the earth. These, along with Zechariah, know that it is "not by might, nor by power, but by [God's] Spirit" (Zech. 4:6, KJV). A total reliance upon that Spirit yields a God-honored simplicity.

Second, God honors sacrifice more than affluence. Our lives become complicated when we acquire gadgets and luxuries. A considerable amount of time and energy is required to locate, pay for, and maintain such items. Also, people become confused, asking themselves whether we are committed to God or to our possessions.

I've always been impressed by the "loose grasp" John Wesley had on things. It wasn't that he made little money. He earned more than most people of eighteenth-century England. Rather, his secret is contained in his philosophy of money: "Money and I have never been the closest of friends. The truth is, we are scarcely passing acquaintances. I've always made it a practice to make all I can to

5. Gayle D. Erwin, *The Jesus Style* (Palm Springs, Calif.: Ronald N. Haynes Publishers, 1983), pp. 18–20.

save all I can to give all I can."[6] And give he did—to the education of ministers, construction of churches, betterment of the poor. His standard of living was never raised, so that each increase in salary meant more money for God's causes.

How much is it possible to live without? The families of one church decided to experiment, living on an average budget of a Third-World family. They planned to do this for one month. Drastic measures were called for: walking and riding bicycles instead of using the car; extending food supplies by using plenty of carbohydrates (e.g., macaroni) instead of meats; unplugging appliances and using candles rather than lights. The results were devastating.

Bickering occurred as individuals battled for their fair share. Many began to cheat, sneaking more than the rules allowed. Some had severe health problems. As a result, the experiment had to be discontinued after two weeks. Even in this limited way, identification with the Third World's plight could not be realized.

Perhaps it should not be realized. Little is gained by being subjected to such destitution, especially when you're not used to its dangerous effects. Also, maybe being comfortable and modestly sustained is not sinful. It is possible to overstate the case against having physical resources.

As a carpenter, Jesus was probably from the middle class of Galilee. Although he was often among the poor, he frequently interacted with those with considerable means. He dined at the banquet tables of wealthy Pharisees (Luke 7:36). Joseph of Arimathea (Matt. 27:57) and Nicodemus (John 19:39), who became disciples of our Lord, were wealthy.

By no means was Jesus a rigid ascetic. His enemies accused him of being a glutton and drunkard (Luke 7:34)—a malicious, exaggerated charge. Yet, he did enjoy joyous

6. This quote is transcribed from a taped performance of D. Paul Thomas, who dramatized Wesley's life in a play entitled *A Heart Strangely Warmed.*

celebrations like a wedding festival (John 2:1–2). He allowed perfume worth a year's wages to be poured over his
head and feet while the disciples grumbled about the needs
of the poor (Matt. 26:6–12).

Nevertheless, acceptance of such persons and circumstances does not mean that our Lord failed to see the dangers of wealth. His parable of the rich farmer pointed to
the dangers of hoarding. Jesus called the farmer a "fool"
(Luke 12:16–21). The Master waged war against the materialism of his day by declaring, "Watch out! Be on your
guard against all kinds of greed; a man's life does not con-
sist in the abundance of his possessions" (Luke 12:15). He
also said, "You cannot serve God and mammon" (Matt.
6:24, KJV). Wealth is a rival god![7]

Our Lord's teaching is clear. Without trying to call attention to ourselves, we must live simply. Amassing a
fortune in order to hoard and gloat, and in spite of global
starvation, is not a worthy life ambition. It deprives the
desperate others with whom we must share.[8] Also, it shows
the world wherein our security lies. It builds walls rather
than bridges between ourselves and the less affluent. How
much better is it to follow the widow's example and make
our giving to God truly sacrificial (Mark 12:42–43). And,
as Paul adds, to do so cheerfully (2 Cor. 9:7).

Third, we honor our heavenly Father more when we
offer sincere thanksgiving rather than when we make constant demands. The other day my friend, Inez, approached
me with a big smile and said, "I've had this unbelievable
problem for the last year. It has caused me anguish." I

7. Richard J. Foster, *Freedom of Simplicity* (San Francisco: Harper and
Row, 1981), pp. 40, 42.
8. What good would result if Christians shared even 10 percent more than
they do currently. Christians worldwide annually earn 6.5 trillion dollars and
own two-thirds of this planet's resources. Their average income is $4,500 per
year, three times that of non-Christians. But, there are more than two hundred
million Christians in the grip of poverty. Increased generosity on our part
would help these and non-Christians who suffer so greatly. (Statistics are from
the *World Christian Almanac*.)

asked the question she seemed eager to answer: "Why do you look so happy and peaceful now?" Her reply: "Because I finally decided to quit nagging God and start thanking him. And that has made all the difference in the world!"

David tells us to "delight [ourselves] in the LORD and he will give [us] the desires of [our] heart" (Ps. 37:4). And when we do purposely delight, it is miraculous how God transforms our desires. We begin wanting most what we most need: his presence in our life. Our genuine thankfullness allows him to generously fill us with that presence.

Paul tells us to "rejoice in the Lord always." To emphasize the point he adds, "I will say it again: Rejoice!" (Phil. 4:4). We ask Paul, "What about the times we're under severe stress?" He declares, "Do not be anxious about anything, but in everything, by prayer and petition, with thanksgiving, present your requests to God" (v. 6). We reply, "Yes—yes—don't keep us in suspense. If we do this, what can we expect?" Again Paul furnishes the answer: "And the peace of God, which transcends all understanding, will guard your hearts and your minds in Christ Jesus" (v. 7).[9]

Begging, pleading, and coaxing God to respond to our laundry list of requests makes prayer complex. When we do so, we visualize him as reluctant to help. As a result, we find ourselves groping for enough convincing arguments, impressive words, and biblical promises to change his attitude toward our plight.

Such an approach is not one of simple faith. This kind of faith Paul urges us to have when he reminds us that we are sons of God, inhabited by the Spirit of his Son. As his sons, we must relate to him as our loving Father (Gal. 4:5-7; Rom. 8:15; the word *Abba* means "daddy" in today's parlance). That is why the writer to the Hebrews

9. Earl G. Lee, *The Cycle of Victorious Living* (Kansas City, Mo.: Beacon Hill, 1971), pp. 28–33. Lee seems to equate "purposeful delight" with thanksgiving. He employs an acrostic to explain the meaning of delight: *D*aily *E*verything *L*aid *I*nto *G*od's *H*ands *T*riumphantly.

says, "Let us then approach the throne of grace with confidence, so that we may receive mercy and find grace to help us in our time of need" (4:16). We know that he is more eager and willing to respond than even our own earthly father (Matt. 7:11; Luke 11:13).

Offering thanksgiving is a surpeme act of worship. Demanding, accompanied by a spirit of doubt, is an act of desperation, a desperation that makes everything seem too complex and confusing.

However, the heartfelt expression of thanksgiving is not limited to words. The scene is the Boston shoreline. An event occurs, without fail, each day at about the same time. An old man appears carrying a bucket full of fresh shrimp. The seagulls are quick to spot their friend and flock to his feet. Some are bold enough to hop on his shoulders. A wide grin breaks out on his face as he feeds them all the shrimp. They thoroughly enjoy a connoisseur seagull's delight!

People used to observe the daily ritual in amazement. Many shook their heads in disgust and thought: What a shame to waste expensive shrimp on the birds! But that was before they learned this story.

The man had been a famous admiral of the American forces in World War II. The Germans torpedoed and sunk his ship, but he and a few of his men managed to climb into a lifeboat. In that cramped vessel they floated for many days, enduring the scorching sun, storms, and a scarcity of food. The men began to die, one by one, until only a few remained, including the admiral. Then came the day that he became dizzy and collapsed. Starvation was near. But while he was lying there, his glassy eyes focused on a small white object next to him. It was a seagull. And it didn't move. His weak and trembling hand slowly reached out and took hold of the gull's foot. It was to become his "manna from heaven," providing enough nourishment to remain alive a few more hours. But that was just long enough to sight an island, where safety was found.

Today, people no longer blame the admiral for providing an expensive banquet for Boston's seagulls. Now they understand. His is a simple act of humble gratitude. Every piece of shrimp offered says "thank you" to God and his feathered friends.

But the admiral's thankful spirit was born of adversity. Is it possible to be thankful in the midst of abundance? I once heard a Thanksgiving Day speaker say, "All that's necessary for us to be unthankful is to have what we need." True indeed. At such times we are tempted even to nag God for luxuries.

It is time to cease clamoring and begin thanking—daily, momentarily, for big blessings, for small ones, in big ways, but also in small ways—like the admiral.

The biblical way of simplicity yields Christian excellence. How can we find that way? We need to acknowledge our weakness, become truly sacrificial, and remember to be genuinely thankful.

But how does this three-part biblical admonition translate into our individual Christian life? Is there a set pattern that we should follow?

Different Steps to the Same Drummer

While I was Dean of Students at a small Christian school in Ohio, I visited a nearby Amish community. I was impressed by the sameness. There was simplicity, but it was the carbon-copy kind. All the houses were white, with look-alike furniture and blue curtains. Every man wore a beard and dressed in black with a wide-brim hat. Each woman donned a bonnet, shawl, apron, and *halsduch* (kerchief). And everyone was transported in the same style black buggy pulled by horses. While respecting their sincerity, I came away questioning their wisdom in forcing everyone into the same mold.

Our God created rich diversity throughout his glorious creation. Like the flowers, birds, and snowflakes, we are all created differently in gifts, temperaments, talents. Our God desires to tailor-make his grace to fit our unique existence so that we can increasingly realize our full potential as we are and where we are. Simplicity is, indeed, our biblical ideal, but not the kind which demands rubber-stamp sameness. What is simple to one may be complex to another. Nevertheless, some suggestions might be helpful, provided we prayerfully adapt them to our unique circumstances. The suggestions fit into two categories: internal and external simplicity.

Internal Simplicity

Find time each day to humbly meditate upon God's Word and seek his guidance in fervent prayer.

Fast at least once each week, without telling others. Use the money for a good cause and the time for meditation.

Periodically make a thank-you list to God, enumerating recent blessings, whether they be great or small. Construct another list of requests that, by faith, you believe God is responding to.

Read one good Christian book each week. Balance your reading list with books that challenge as well as books that comfort.

Write something in your spiritual diary each day. It can be in the form of a letter to God.

Practice the presence of Christ. Imagine that Jesus is by your side throughout the day. Begin with one hour, then gradually increase your time of awareness.

Ask a trusted Christian friend to tell you of your faults in a spirit of Christian love. Reject the temptation to be defensive or discouraged. Realize that God offers to be your partner in improvement.

Cultivate the ability to truly worship every moment you are in a worship service. Fervent prayer, concentrating on the words of songs, and taking notes on sermons can be helpful.

Memorize key passages in God's Word or the words of inspirational hymns.

Strive to glean a spiritual lesson out of situations that occur in the course of a day (e.g., at the laundromat, concentrate on the importance of "washing" in the Scriptures).

External Simplicity

As often as God leads, give away something to which you are strongly attached. Preferably, you should give anonymously to someone in need.

Give a faith gift (beyond your means) to God's kingdom, whether it be to a church, Christian college, or missionary cause. Promise God that amount when (not if) he provides it—believing that he will.

Continually suggest ways that your church can be less "building and facility conscious" and be more "people conscious." If people do not respond, dare to reapportion your church giving as an example.

Refuse to purchase gaudy luxuries for the sake of being "seen of men." Do not reject buying quality items, but reject fads and overpriced brands.

Plan to use cars, clothing, and appliances for a longer period of time. Much that is thought to be out of date is perfectly usable.

Do more bicycle riding and walking. It is healthy and sets an example for being a good steward of God's resources.

Minimize your reliance upon costly, empty-caloried junk food. Also, in regards to meat, favor that which swims (fish) and has wings (chicken). Reasons: health and cost.

Dedicate one "big-gift" day (e.g., birthday, Christmas) to others in need. Instead of exchanging with another, or receiving many presents from others, request all parties to give to a needy cause.

Make it known to all family members that you are willing a substantial portion of your estate to God's kingdom. Explain the reasons.

Periodically give up comforts for a span of time (e.g., air conditioning, television, eating out, customary vacations).

The prayerful cultivation of simplicity is every Christian's business. And as it is increasingly experienced, its untold value is increasingly seen. May we apply its principles to our life, as we seek to travel a more excellent journey. These principles are reflected in an inspiring poem by William Ellery Channing:

My Symphony

I will seek elegance rather than luxury,
    refinement rather than fashion.

I will seek to be worthy more than respectable,
    wealthy and not rich.

I will study hard, think quietly,
    talk gently, act frankly.

I will listen to stars and birds,
    babes and sages, with an open heart.

I will bear all things cheerfully, do all things
    bravely, await occasions and hurry never.

In a word I will let the spiritual, unbidden
    and unconscious grow up through the common.[10]

---

10. The poem is transcribed from a taped sermon of the Reverend Lamar Kincaid, who spoke at Longboat Key Chapel, Longboat Key, Florida, in 1973.

Keep yourself clean and bright, for you are the window through which you must see the world. — George Bernard Shaw

Who will tell you the truth? An enemy who hates you bitterly, and a friend who loves you dearly. —Anonymous

We readily confess our little faults in order to suggest that we have no big ones. —François de La Rochefoucauld

Do you know why the man who operates on people wears a mask? So if he really messes up, the patient won't know who did it. —Small boy to playmate

8

The Joy of Unmasking

Have you ever known an honest-to-goodness "mystery man," a Howard-Hughes-type character?

I've encountered only one such person. He has become a legend in his own time. This fellow spends his vast riches in erratic ways, constantly travels throughout the world and, when least expected, pops up at a social event for a cameo appearance. Whenever he appears, he seems to look completely different. A human chameleon!

Talk about mystery, this fellow invented it. There are all sorts of wild tales about his antics. But most stories focus on his benevolence. Mr. X gives great amounts to needy causes. Perhaps this is why so many admire him, much as the early Californians admired Death Valley

Scotty, who often threw bushels of dollar bills to crowds from the window of his private train.

It was a beautiful fall day when we boarded the plane for the Hawaiian Islands. My wife had managed to acquire another "deal" through her travel agency. We located our seats and buckled in. It was then that we noticed a slovenly-looking man in the front cabin area. Suddenly he grabbed the stewardess, took her to the row where we were seated, and demanded that a fragile-looking lady get out of his seat. (She had moved over after the door was closed, assuming the seat was vacant.) The embarrassed stewardess kindly requested the frightened lady to move.

After taking his seat, the insistent man began making life miserable for everyone in the row, including us. He loudly complained whenever anyone needed to step by him, laughed uncontrollably at the movie, and intimidated the woman he had so discourteously ejected.

At first he looked familiar, but I quickly suppressed the thought. I hoped that I didn't recognize him. Then my unconscious mind produced an undeniable recall. It was the "mystery man," the same person considered by so many to be gracious and generous, the epitome of gentlemanly kindness.

In those five hours of flying, Mr. X went from being a candidate for sainthood to being my nominee for Mr. Obnoxious of the Decade! He never did recognize the two of us. Consequently, at social occasions where we've since seen him, he is once again disguised as Mr. Nice Guy.

How can this man maintain two fiercely competing identities? His life must be extremely complex.

Masks Too Good to Lose

We've all encountered persons like Mr. X, people who display a respectable image around those they seek to impress, but the opposite with those they consider insignificant. Such individuals have mastered the devious art of mask wearing.

But *all* mask wearing is not bad. In fact, in some situations, mask wearing can be fun. Going to a party dressed like a clown or ghost is an example. We delight in assuming the role of another for a few hours, especially if everyone is costumed.

And what about seeing a favorite play where performers skillfully assume the identities of various characters? We do not berate the actors because they have set aside their true selves. Instead, their "legitimate hypocrisy" can be entertaining and admirable.[1]

Furthermore, our daily lives demand a certain amount of role-playing. In *As You Like It* (II. vii.), William Shakespeare declared:

> All the world's a stage,
> And all the men and women merely players:
> They have their exits and their entrances;
> And one man in his time plays many parts.

We must all do things we don't feel like doing—go to work with a headache, be friendly with those we dislike, or fix a flat tire in our best clothes. We force ourselves to carry out such distasteful assignments.

Also, we must constantly change masks to adapt to different situations. We wouldn't dare speak to our boss as we do to our children. Nor would we act in church as we do at a ball game. As "civilized" persons, we know

1. Charles R. Swindoll relates an interesting connection between the mask and the generic term for "hypocrite" in the ancient Greek plays. "Did you know that the word 'hypocrite' comes from the ancient Greek plays? An actor would place a large, grinning mask in front of his face and quote his comedy lines as the audience would roar with laughter. He would then slip backstage and grab a frowning, sad, oversized mask and come back quoting tragic lines as the audience would moan and weep. Guess what he was called. A *hypocritos*, one who wears a mask." Charles R. Swindoll, *Improving Your Serve: The Art of Unselfish Living* (Waco: Word, 1981), p. 117.

that we must constantly change our performances. Every situation has its own rules to which we must conform. Few people like rebels. Persons who insist on "making waves" are generally rejected.[2]

Social psychologist George Herbert Mead made a distinction between two parts of the "self": "I," the private, innermost person, and "me," the role-playing, mask-wearing part of self that adapts to others' expectations. According to Mead, if we are to be well-adjusted adults, we will develop a healthy "me" as well as a robust "I." To "do our own thing" in spite of all can only spell catastrophe. Role playing cannot be discarded or ignored.[3]

In summary, role playing is vital to our well-being and can even bring enjoyment to our lives. It is essential, in spite of what many well-meaning Christian writers have said.[4] There is truly a sense in which we must be "in the flow" of society, in the world, although not of it.

Masks That Pinch Our Faces

Nevertheless, as we saw in the case of Mr. X, role playing can get out of hand. It can damage us and harm those

2. This fact we demonstrated in a social psychological experiment in which ten small groups of paid participants were gathered for problem-solving exercises. A "confederate" (a person in on the secret) was placed in each group, with instructions to mildly disagree with the consensus. Then all group members were asked to vote on one person who should be eliminated due to a shortage of funds. In all ten groups, the "winner" was the person who "made waves."

3. See George Herbert Mead, *Mind, Self, and Society: From the Standpoint of a Social Behaviorist* (Chicago: University of Chicago Press, 1934). The same theme is presented in Erving Goffman, *The Presentation of Self in Everyday Life* (New York: Anchor, 1959).

4. Christian writers often make the general statement: "We must get rid of all masks." The opening sentence in a book by Charles R. Swindoll is: "Okay, everybody, masks off!" *Dropping Your Guard: The Value of Open Relationships* (Waco: Word, 1983), p. 9. The beginning psychology or social psychology student knows that the complete and indiscriminate stripping of defense mechanisms is extremely dangerous. Mask peeling is a much more complicated undertaking than many Christian (or non-Christian) writers realize or admit.

with whom we associate. Under what conditions does role playing go sour?

When the "me" overtakes the "I" we're in trouble. We must always be more than our performance. There is a kernel self that must be continuously cultivated and protected. And that self must be balanced against the role-playing part of our personality. Scores of movie and sports stars have allowed their social images to smother their private selves. As a result, they sometimes rely on alcohol or drugs, or commit suicide.

Our masks must be consistent. To act too far out of character, even at a masquerade party, is distasteful and unwise. Recall that Mr. X became a completely different person when he perceived himself to be anonymous. Role playing must be guided by consistent values and attitudes. To be compassionate, then harsh; jovial, then depressive; scrupulously fair, then radically dishonest cannot be tolerated within the role behavior of the same individual. Some variation is healthy, but extremes must be avoided.

Although role playing for purposes of cooperation is often commendable, that which intends to deceive, hurt, or acquire undeserved gain is to be soundly rejected. Recall the resentment we've all felt after buying an overpriced, unreliable product because it was misrepresented by a convincing salesperson! Don't slip on a new mask in order to take advantage of another person. To do so cultivates cynicism throughout our society.

Finally, wearing masks in order to hide deep insecurities is unacceptable. To do so is to reject making improvement. Also, it means that we perceive ourselves as unworthy. Our inner being cries out to be revealed in order to be accepted. We must respond to that cry in spite of the risk.

In summary, masks that bury the inner self, masks that are radically inconsistent, masks that attempt to deceive, and masks that hide deeply ingrained insecurities must be rejected! They must be peeled off continuously, for they have a way of growing back. To keep them off our faces is to know the liberating feeling of being open, transparent, and having first-hand knowledge of sincerity and honesty. Few things can compare with that.

This feeling of openness is much like taking a bath, pulling up the shade to let the sunshine in, or breathing country air. Also, it's knowing what it really means to have a satisfying measure of Christian excellence. Such openness allows the love of God to flow freely from ourselves to others. The barriers are removed and the floodgates are opened. Pure love can now pour forth as God intended!

Most of us are aware of the danger of wearing the wrong kind of masks. On others they look grotesque. On ourselves we feel that our God-created identity is totally camouflaged, submerged in an ocean of deceit. Why do we persist in wearing such masks?

Why We Play Damaging Roles

Although none of us is exactly alike, we tend to gravitate toward the damaging kind of role playing for the same reasons.

First, some of us follow the example of one (or both) of our parents. It seems to come naturally, and ever more so as we get older. If, for example, our father was a hypocrite, we will usually tend to resemble him.[5] I cannot help but think of child evangelist Marjoe Gortner, whose con-artist father threatened to drown him in bath water unless he memorized his sermons to perfection. That he did, for I witnessed one of his "performances" as a child in the late 1940s. With his kind of parental guidance, it is little won-

---

5. Parental influence is great. The strongest correlation, for example, related to child-abuse is whether you were beaten by your own parents. There are two predominant reactions: reactance (i.e., acting the opposite of one's parents) and compliance (i.e., responding as one's parents would). The latter is far more likely than the former, especially as one becomes older.

der that he told *Time:* "I can't think of a time that I ever believed in God." But that disbelief didn't stop him from preaching for profit, long after leaving his mercenary parents. He was drawn to his father's teaching and example.[6]

Second, we wear masks in order to avoid painful consequences. To "face the music," to "take your licks," to "bite the bullet" is not delightful. So we fake it. Attempting not to look stupid, we use long Latin words instead of short Anglo-Saxon ones. Trying to look different than the poor person we are, we buy a few name-brand items to fool the world. We especially grope for our masks when we know we're guilty and someone might lower the boom. I mused about the letter a university student sent to her parents:

> Dear Mom and Dad:
> I'm sorry to be so long in writing. Unfortunately all my stationary was destroyed the night our dorm was set fire by the demonstrators. I'm out of the hospital now, and the doctor says my eyesight should return—sooner or later. The wonderful boy, Bill, who rescued me from the fire kindly offered to share his little apartment with me until the dorm is rebuilt. He comes from a good family—so you won't be surprised when I tell you we are going to be married. In fact, since you always wanted a grandchild, you'll be glad to know that you'll be grandparents next month!
> P.S. Please disregard the above practice in English composition. There was no fire. I haven't been in the hospital. I'm not pregnant. And I don't have a steady boyfriend. But—I *did* get a "D" in French and an "F" in Chemistry, and *I just wanted to be sure you received this news in the proper perspective.*

We also wear the wrong kind of masks to benefit from the status of another person. When we believe ourselves to be unworthy, we often ride piggyback on the identity

6. "Hollow Holiness," *Time,* 14 August 1972, p. 45.

of another self, even if that person is a product of our imagination. When mentally ill individuals resort to this, we describe them as having multiple personalities or hallucinations.[7] When we do it in a less pronounced manner, it is simply known as playing the role. Usually it is closely related to such things as fads, trends, crazes, and modeling.[8]

The temptation to imitate another individual is powerful. Ministers find themselves copying the style of Billy Graham or Robert Schuller. Appearance-conscious Americans mimic the dress and hair styles of Robert Redford or Diana, Princess of Wales, and I'd like to have a quarter for every teen-ager wearing a glove just like Michael Jackson's. Then there's the recent exhibit of the Mona Lisa in Tokyo. Many Japanese girls had plastic surgery to become permanent, although inexact, replicas of the lady with the famous smile! There is no end to the variety of masks that people will enthusiastically wear in order to gain a little borrowed self-esteem.

Finally, some well-intentioned people wear masks in order to cushion others from the crushing impact of harsh realities. Far from being malicious, such role playing is intended to soften life's blows by casting a more positive light on another's painful situation, whether it be incurable cancer, loss of employment, or outright rejection of a dream.

Every author fears his archfoe, the rejection slip. Realizing that he must be told when he is turned down, he still doesn't relish hearing that he is incompetent. He wants to be told in a nice way. An aspiring author in China was sent a rejection note from his government:

We have read your manuscript with boundless delight. But

7. Kenneth Bianchi, the so-called Hillside Strangler, has been diagnosed as having multiple personalities. As Kenneth, he is a soft-spoken, courteous gentleman. But as Steve, he is a merciless murderer and sex pervert.

8. See Jon Johnston, *Will Evangelicalism Survive Its Own Popularity?* (Grand Rapids: Zondervan, 1980), chap. 6, pp. 103–22.

if we were to publish your paper, it would be impossible for us to publish work of lower standard. And as it is unthinkable that, in the next three thousand years, we shall see its equal, we are regretfully compelled to return your divine composition. We beg you a thousand times to overlook our short sight and timidity.

What a contrast to the sign I recently spotted in a grocery store:

> All Shoplifters Will Be Merrily
> Beaten to a Bloody Pulp!

Both of these are insincere. The messages are exaggerated. The former is an inflated evaluation. The latter relies on brutal frankness for the purpose of humor. As Christians, we must find a middle ground. We must be both candid and sensitive, honest and compassionate. This is no easy task.

In attempting to balance reality with others' feelings, I have often been tempted to soften the truth. And it has been easy for me to rationalize. After all, aren't the feelings of people more important than principles? An affirmative answer to this has left me feeling justified in donning masks that shade the truth.

Although this issue hasn't been totally resolved in my mind and heart, I'm beginning to see dangers related to even this kind of mask wearing. There is always the chance that people will discover the real facts and hold me accountable for not "coming clean." In addition, it seems as though I am tempted to continue faking it, even after realizing that the whole truth would no longer hurt the person(s) involved. To represent the facts is to risk losing face and destroying confidence.

It is vital that we understand the kinds of masks that exist—both harmless and harmful. In addition, we must fully comprehend the underlying reasons we wear our disguises. To do so is to take a giant step toward God's kind of openness, the kind that benefits the excellent Christian!

Let's explore what God's Word says about altering one's identity.

A Clarion Call to Sincerity

Although the Bible refrains from using the modern-day terms *transparency, openness,* and *unblocked interfacing,* the message comes through that God does not tolerate fakes. His servants must declare with Job of old: "And my tongue will utter no deceit" (27:4b).

The Old Testament reveals how Adam and Eve blatantly sinned and then slipped on the mask of innocence. That was after they had hidden from God. Facing their Maker, and confronted with their sin, Adam blamed Eve and Eve blamed the serpent. God blamed them both and expelled them from the Garden of Eden (Gen. 3:8–17).

Joshua clearly saw through Achan's mask of honesty and discovered that he had stolen spoils of war and hidden them in his tent. His dishonesty had resulted in a costly defeat for Israel's army. Achan was put to death and his property was destroyed (Josh. 7:18–26).

Israel's first king, Saul, pretended that he had been obedient. God commanded that he kill the Amalekites, as well as destroy their property. But Saul spared their wicked king, Agag, and kept the best livestock. Soon thereafter God's prophet, Samuel, informed Saul that God had rejected his kingship (1 Sam. 15:7–22).

New Testament writers emphatically condemn those who live a lie. Paul declared, "Provide things honest in the sight of all men" (Rom. 12:17b, KJV). "Let us walk honestly . . ." (13:13a, KJV). "Provid[e] for honest things, not only in the sight of the Lord, but also in the sight of men" (2 Cor. 8:21, KJV). "Now I pray to God that ye . . . should do that which is honest . . ." (13:7, KJV). In another passage he writes, "I pray . . . that ye may approve things

that are excellent; that ye may be sincere . . ." (Phil. 1:10,
KJV). "He further advises, Whatsoever things are true,
whatsoever things are honest . . .; if there be any virtue
[*aretē*, excellence], . . . think on these things" (4:8, KJV).

In a similar vein, the writer to the Hebrews states, "Pray
for us: for we trust we have a good conscience, in all things
willing to live honestly" (13:18, KJV). Finally, the apostle
Peter admonishes Christians to have honest conversation
among the Gentiles (1 Peter 2:12a).

But, as with the other attributes of Christian excellence,
we must look to the incarnate One as our model. Was
sincerity a theme of his life and teaching?

In a key messianic passage of Isaiah, the prophet pre-
dicted that our Lord would be characterized by total honesty. In his inspired vision he declared, "Nor was any
deceit in his mouth" (53:9). Never was there a more accurate prediction. Our Lord never said anything he didn't
believe, profess anything he didn't feel, nor lay claim to
anything he didn't possess!

Centuries have passed since his resurrection, and many
uncomplimentary statements have been made about our
Savior. He has been called a visionary, fanatic, dreamer.
But amazingly few have labeled Jesus an intentional de-
ceiver. As Charles Edward Jefferson declares, "There is
something so pure and frank and noble about him that to
doubt his sincerity would be like doubting the brightness
of the sun."[9]

Because Jesus embodied sincerity, he could not hold
back the claim that he was the Good Shepherd (John 10:11,
14), the Door (10:7), the Bread of Life (6:35), and the Light
of the World (8:12)—even though he knew it would cost
him his life. But he had to say it, because it was (and is)
the absolute truth!

Jesus' incorruptible honesty prompted an outpouring of

9. Charles Edward Jefferson, *The Character of Jesus* (New York: Grosset
and Dunlap, 1908), p. 64.

candid words from his lips. To the Pharisees, who wore imbedded masks of self-righteousness, he declared, "You belong to your father, the devil . . . a murderer from the beginning . . . and the father of lies" (John 8:44). This is certainly not the language of the counterfeit humble, the timid, or the politically-minded. It is the language of God's only begotten Son.

And Jesus demanded his kind of honesty from his followers. For example, in a day when people hid behind all sorts of oaths, he commanded that his disciples refrain from all swearing.[10] His words are plain and direct: "Simply let your 'Yes' be 'Yes,' and your 'No,' 'No'; anything beyond this comes from the evil one" (Matt. 5:37).

This is the Man we want and need, for he is our refuge in the time of storm. When we are deceived and disappointed, we can find comfort in the One who says, "I am . . . the truth" (John 14:6). When we are weary and confused, we can rest our souls upon One who is more faithful than the stars. His voice inspires assurance and quenches all uncertainty and doubt. He soothes and heals us by being genuine!

What he teaches about God we can receive. What he says about the soul we can believe. What he declares about sin and its penalty we can accept. What he proclaims about the victorious life we need never doubt. When he instructs us to do something we can proceed, assured that it is the best thing to do. When he warns against a course

10. The religious leaders of Jesus' time categorized "oaths" as binding or nonbinding. An oath containing the name of God was thought to be obligatory throughout life. But if another name was used, a person could break the oath. As Jefferson states, "Jesus was disgusted by the reasoning of the bat-eyed pettifoggers." In this Scripture he implied if you want to stress something, simply say it again. If people still don't get the message, quietly repeat it. "The world should be a place where all the evidence needed to prove something true is that a man asserts it. Today's courts of justice demand oaths because Satan has corrupted hearts and rendered ordinary speech unreliable." Ibid., pp. 59–60.

of action we can shun it, knowing that it will lead to destruction.

That is why, as his followers, growing in his excellence, we feel increasingly secure and satisfied with our Lord. Our hearts become evermore at peace as they rest upon the One who is completely sincere.

Results We Can Expect

As we grow closer to the Master, and learn of him (Matt. 11:28–30), we begin possessing his kind of genuineness. What does that mean in practical, everyday terms?

We have a self-concept that becomes progressively healthy and positive. We come to see ourselves through the loving eyes of the One who was crucified for us. And as this occurs, we loosen our death grip on our damaging masks. Rather, we unashamedly desire to reveal more of a self that we have come to increasingly respect.[11]

With inner confidence, we realize that our unmasking need not rely on being with a group of unmaskers who meet for that sole purpose. Some people become extremely dependent on a closed, intimate group that cultivates deep introspection and revelation. Innermost secrets are shared. Emotions are given free reign—even to the point of such things as the primal scream. After laying bare their souls, such participants (sometimes called "groupie-bums") become locked into a dependence on the group.

Unlike this kind of emotional "unclothing," biblical unmasking is not restricted to a set time period with unmaskers. Nor does it advocate unmasking for the mere sake of it, leaving the human psyche unprotected and vulnerable to a rigid group dependency. Rather, our masks

11. See Jon Johnston, "Symptoms of a Lack of Self-esteem," in *Building Self-esteem*, ed. Gene Van Note (Kansas City, Mo.: Beacon Hill, 1983), pp. 14–21.

are taken off in order to put on Christ! As Paul so aptly states, "You have taken off your old self . . . and have put on the new self, which is being renewed in knowledge in the image of its Creator. . . . Christ is all, and is in all" (Col. 3:9–11).

The Holy Spirit increasingly helps us to discern which masks are harmful. As we previously discussed, some disguises are harmless while others are crippling. Therefore, all mask shedding must involve a careful obedience to his guidance.

As J. Kenneth Grider declared, every Christian should maintain a core of privacy. We need not feel compelled to reveal everything about ourselves. For example, it can be damaging to constantly disclose details about our preconversion life of sin. With the psalmist we can take comfort that "as far as the east is from the west, so far has he removed our transgressions from us" (103:12). There's no need to dwell on our precleansed identity, nor to willfully shatter the confidence of others by continuous revelations about our sordid past.

On the other hand, the Holy Spirit will guide us to peel off masks that cultivate unspiritual phoniness and outright deceit.

Finally, that same Holy Spirit will progressively inform us as to who should receive our revelation, and when. Certain people can be devastated by our complete unmasking. Others, with Satan's help, can be counted on to use newfound information against us as they twist the facts in a degrading manner.

Still others need for our relationship with them to deepen before they can benefit from our candid revelations. My wife knew a woman for a brief period. Suddenly this woman decided that she wanted to become an intimate friend—instantly. At their next meeting, she turned to my startled wife and announced, "I want to be your friend, and we can never really be friends until you tell me everything about yourself! Do it now." I assure you, her request was not granted and for good reason. Relationships require time. So should self-disclosure. But, again, God has provided his Spirit to guide us into knowing if (and when) disclosures should be made. We can rely on that with certainty.

It's All in a Name

To call ourselves Christian is to say much about the kind of identity we claim, or it should. The term implies "miniature Christ": being saturated with his presence and nature, so that we come to perceive human existence and relate to all persons as he did. That means manifesting sincerity and genuineness. To not do this is to take his name in vain.

It was reported to Alexander the Great that one of his soldiers, who also happened to be named Alexander, needed to be soundly disciplined for bad behavior. The soldier was dispatched to the great conquerer's presence. He was asked to confess and hastily did. After hearing the shameful admissions, Alexander turned to his namesake and made one simple statement: "Soldier, either change your conduct or change your name!" The same admonition applies to those of us who bear the name of our Lord. May complete honesty characterize our lives!

People are not looking for a friendly church as much as they are looking for a friend. —Bill M. Sullivan

Relationships are built up, like a fine lacquer finish, with the layers of kindness. —Alan Loy McGinnis

You cannot sprinkle the perfume of happiness on someone else without spilling a few drops on yourself. —Leo Charles Johnston, Sr.

How many Californians are required to change a light bulb? Five. One to do the work, and four to relate with him in the experience. —Anonymous

9

Webs of Love

It's tough to be left out, excluded, overlooked, or neglected. When it happens, it is often hard to forget.

I recall trying out for P.O.N.Y. League baseball as a boy. Someone had observed my playing skills at a sand-lot game and suggested that I go for the "big time."

I could visualize it all: home runs, cheering crowds, perhaps even a major league baseball contract in a few years. My parents would be so proud of their son—the same parents I was presently requesting to purchase all the paraphernalia needed to play: glove, uniform, shoes.

The coach of my team was a Christian. He was eager for me to do well, so that I might be a positive influence on the other fellows. That is why he gave me every chance possible. I was on the starting line-up in the first game.

Then my balloon popped. The dream vanished. I began what seemed like an endless string of strike-outs. Everyone tried to advise me, but things didn't improve. The poor coach continued to play me, to his chagrin. I did okay in practice—it was daytime. But under the glaring lights, before the boisterous crowd, my performance was pitiful. Finally, even my patient coach was forced to face reality. He had the team to think about. I had to be replaced immediately!

The skipper broke it to me gently, but my hurt was intense. I was being asked to sit in the dugout and watch my teammates play the game I loved. To cease being an enthusiastic, full participant. To become a mere pinch hitter, which really meant being an uninvolved spectator. The message was clear: I was no longer a part of the team. Banished to the bench!

It was painful to even look in the faces of the other players. They were well aware of my demotion and realized that I was no longer a participating member of their team. It wasn't long before I could take the rejection no more. I turned in my uniform—and with it my dreams.

But in retrospect, my situation wasn't nearly as bad as it seemed. My performance merited my exclusion. I had been given my chance. Also, I did have the option of quitting. Often in life, people must continue under the dark cloud of rejection. The apostle Paul was such a person.

No Welcome Mat

For well over a decade after his conversion, Paul was not fully accepted by his church. Shortly after being born again on the Damascas road,[1] and after being filled with

---

1. J. Kenneth Grider offers references to substantiate that Saul (Paul) did receive his conversion on the Damascus Road. It is implied that he was entirely sanctified three days later with Ananias. Something revolutionary occurred when Saul saw the heavens light up, fell to the ground, and conversed with the risen Christ. He immediately ceased being the main persecutor of Christians (Acts 9:3–6). He was called as a "chosen" (eklogēs, a Greek word having salvation overtones) instrument to preach the gospel. And he was so called on the Damascus road before seeing Ananias (Acts 9:15). Saul twice called Christ "Lord" (Kurie, Acts 9:5; 22:8), using the identical Greek word used by the

the Holy Spirit before Ananias, he began preaching in the synagogues of Damascus—"baffl[ing] the Jews ... by proving that Jesus is the Christ" (Acts 9:22). Then he went to Jerusalem, where the disciples "were all afraid of him, not believing that he really was a disciple" (v. 26).

The disciples finally agreed to take a wait-and-see attitude only after Barnabas testified that Paul had "preached fearlessly in the name of Jesus" (v. 27). Undaunted, the apostle left Jerusalem to blaze a missionary trail for his Lord—starting churches, writing letters of inspiration, proclaiming the Good News. He encountered all sorts of persecution: prison, flogging, shipwreck, hunger (see 2 Cor. 11:23b–30).

After three years Paul once again decided to become part of the "team." So off to Jerusalem he trekked, "to get acquainted with Peter" (Gal. 1:18). Although he stayed with Peter for fifteen days, he "saw none of the other apostles—only James, the Lord's brother." Talk about cold treatment! Paul undeservedly received it!

But there was no quitting for the apostle, although Satan no doubt tempted him to become discouraged. He traveled again. Congregations were organized. People were gloriously converted from all walks of life. But he did encounter problems along the way: outright rejection and persecution from the Jews and biting suspicion from Jewish Christians who knew Paul only as "persecutor turned preacher." For all the latter knew, he might reverse himself and once again begin persecuting them.

---

full-fledged Christian, Ananias (Acts 9:10). Ananias approached Saul and called him "brother" (Acts 9:17). In so doing, he told him, at the outset, that he considered him to already be a fellow Christian believer. Their encounter did not involve "conversion language." Ananias specifically told Saul that Christ has sent him so that he (Saul) might "see again and be filled with the Holy Spirit" (Acts 9:17). In conclusion Grider adds, "Of numerous commentators checked, almost none of them, whatever their doctrinal stance, take the position that [this] conversion did not occur on the Damascus Road." *Entire Sanctification: The Distinctive Doctrine of Wesleyanism* (Kansas City, Mo.: Beacon Hill, 1980), pp. 46–48.

It wasn't until fourteen years later (seventeen after his conversion) that the missionary from Tarsus returned to Jerusalem with Barnabas and Titus. They went to discuss the issue of Gentile circumcision with the church leaders. For the first time Paul received complete acceptance. He joyfully recorded, "James, Peter and John, those reputed to be pillars, gave me and Barnabas the right hand of fellowship when they recognized the grace given to me" (Gal. 2:9).

But what took them so long? Why the seventeen-year probation period? How could the Jewish early church keep Paul at arms' length when he so desperately reached out for fellowship and acceptance? We can only wonder and ask rhetorical questions.

Like Paul, do we all have a driving need for acceptance, to be part of a "team," rather than just a pinch hitter? Absolutely.

Suffering from Marasmus?

We're all born with a compelling need to belong. Belong we must—if we are to survive.

During World War II, orphaned babies were placed in a large institution. The accommodations were pleasant: new furniture, brightly colored toys, delicious food. Nevertheless, the health of the children began to rapidly deteriorate. Although there were no signs of disease, they stopped eating and playing. They then grew weak and began dying.

United Nations doctors were flown in to investigate. Their prescription: For ten minutes each hour, all children were to be picked up, hugged, kissed, played with, talked to. The orders were obeyed and, within a short time, the strange epidemic disappeared. The little ones brightened. Their appetites returned. Their toys were once again played with. And when their ten minutes came, they enthusiastically reached out their little arms to be picked up by the approaching nurses.

The doctors identified their fatal lethargy as marasmus

and described it as "a mysterious and gradual emaciation of the body which seems to strike when others don't take time to show enough love."[2]

The same principle holds true for the elderly. Social disengagement leads to loneliness and eventual death. Our senior citizens feel the effects of such isolation perhaps more than any other group in our society. No doubt that is why senility is so prevalent and why postretirement life averages only four years. The cry of most older people was voiced to me by my father, shortly after his retirement: "Son, you can criticize me, accuse me, borrow from me, make fun of me all you want—but just don't ever leave me alone."

But we all have an irrepressible need to interact with others. This truth has been said in so many ways. John Dunne states, "No man is an island unto himself." Baruch Spinoza declares, "Man is a social animal." Reuben Welch, in his book by that title, asserts, "We really do need each other."[3] Lloyd Ogilvie says God created us to be riverbeds rather than reservoirs. There must be a constant inflow and outflow of social contact with our lives.[4]

That's why we socialize, converse, give gifts, smile. That's why we join so many organizations, some of which seem humorous:

Let's Have Better Mottoes Association. Its goal is to replace worn-out slogans with creative ones: "It's not whether you win or lose, but how you place the blame."

2. It is a medical fact that if a newborn infant is isolated in a closet for the first weeks of his life, separated from communication and touch, he will suffer irreparable brain damage and even death. Frederick II of Prussia conducted such a grisly experiment, attempting to prove that newborns, if left unattended, will begin speaking Latin on their own. As we might expect, the babies (although provided food and water) perished.

3. Reuben Welch, *We Really Do Need Each Other* (Nashville: Impact, n.d.).

4. The Reverend Lloyd Ogilvie is pastor of the Hollywood (California) Presbyterian Church. The idea was taken from a sermon he presented on one of his national telecasts.

Committee to Award Miss Piggy the Oscar. This group is dedicated to the proposition, in the organization's words, that "all pork bellies are *not* created equal."

Man Will Never Fly Society Internationale. The society maintains that mankind was never meant to wing it. Its motto: "If man were meant to fly, God would have given him propellers!"[5]

And there is much to gain by being sociable. Psychologist James J. Lynch researched the lives of seven thousand persons, ages thirty through sixty-nine, for a period of nine years. His conclusion is that outgoing, sociable individuals live longer and healthier lives than those who are shut off from others. The former are more resistant to heart and circulatory diseases, cancer, and strokes—and are even less inclined to suicide.[6]

People refer to this phenomenon in many ways: assimilation, systemics, linkage, social webbing, or fellowship. But it all comes down to one important idea: We're all born with an insatiable inner need for meaningful interaction with others. This need begins on the first day of our lives. It continues until we breathe our last breath.

What is the significance of this fact for Christians desiring to deepen in biblical excellence?

Fellowship: Keynote in God's Word

The Bible spotlights the concept of fellowship, beginning with the creation account in Genesis. Most of us believe that God created Adam to have fellowship with him. Soon thereafter, Eve was created for Adam—and for the same reason. God said, "It is not good for the man to be alone" (2:18).

5. Steve Lawhead, "Absurd Associations," *Campus Life,* July-August 1982, pp. 36–38.
6. "Socio-Feedback," *Time,* 16 January 1978, n.p.

Then the "first family" of Eden's garden blatantly sinned. Their sin, like any sin, caused their fellowship with God to be broken. Feeling guilty and ashamed, they hid from the presence of the One whose holiness made them feel worse. Their hiding probably hurt our loving heavenly Father more than anything they did.

From this story we glean an important truth: Excellent fellowship depends on excellent character. Our hearts must be right with God and purged of all uncleanness (see chap. 4) before we can lovingly relate with others. In his reference to our fellowship with other Christians, John states, "But if we walk in the light [i.e., become increasingly holy], as he [God] is in the light, we have [his kind of] fellowship with one another . . ." (1 John 1:7).

What a joy it is to relate with those who manifest his purity and love. No wonder it refreshes and uplifts us to meet together with other believers. David declared, "I rejoiced with those who said to me, 'Let us go to the house of the LORD' " (Ps. 122:1).

Aware of its importance, the writer of Hebrews instructs us to "not forsak[e] the assembling of ourselves together . . ." (10:25, KJV). And Jesus promises, ". . . where two or three come together in my name, there am I with them" (Matt. 18:20). Finally, Paul declares, "God . . . has called you into fellowship with his Son Jesus Christ our Lord" (1 Cor. 1:9). Implicit is the idea that Christian fellowship is possible only because of his work within us. Because we are of kindred mind and spirit, our meeting together is special. Something marvelous occurs. The air is electrified with his presence.

Why do we share the Good News of the gospel? John provides the answer: "We proclaim to you [non-Christians] what we have seen and heard, so that you also may have fellowship with us. And our fellowship is with the Father and with his Son, Jesus Christ" (1 John 1:3). In other words, come and join us. His blessings are too good to be enjoyed by a select few. There is an abundance of power, peace, and joy to go around for all who will come and all who will invite his excellent love into their lives.

As excellent Christians, our primary goal in life must be to attract and disciple outsiders into our nourishing fellowship. That is why we are servants, live a simplified lifestyle, and are filled with the Holy Spirit (see Acts 1:8). As God guides us in weaving a "love web" around their hearts, our own love becomes increasingly more excellent.

Giving spiritual birth to one of his creation, for whom his only Son died, transcends the joy of giving biological birth. Or it should. It is like saying to someone lost in sin: "Welcome to an eternity of joy. Meet the greatest people in the world, the *koinōnia*—the fellowship of believers— who are filled with God's own Spirit!"

Unfortunately, drawing sinners into Christian fellowship frequently ranks low on our list of spiritual priorities. No wonder nearly four hundred evangelical Christians are required, each year, to bring one new "spiritual baby" into our fellowship! But why? What sidetracks us from fulfilling the biblical imperative?

Why Webs of Love Aren't Woven

First, we get tangled in our love webs. We fail to distinguish between the urgent (i.e., what clamors for immediate attention) and the necessary (i.e., what is best to do for the long run).

We have a knack for getting lost in trivia and busywork, things that need some attention, but are not critical to kingdom business. In so doing, we're a lot like the man who kept arranging deck furniture on the *Titanic*. He was so busy that he didn't bother to look down at the water and notice that the ship was sinking. Somehow, our priorities are not God's priorities.

All too often our best time and energy are consumed in such maintenance activities, duties that focus on keeping the church doors open: landscaping, repairing, ushering, meeting on boards.

And how could I possibly forget? Singing in the choir. More valuable spiritual energy is consumed in making music for ourselves than perhaps any other area. We've heard the expression *a church with a choir.* I know of one that can, more accurately, be described as a choir with a church. There is no calling program, ministry to shut-ins, street witnessing. But there is a choir filled with people who are convinced that they're fulfilling their total spiritual obligation by performing musically. The deck furniture must be arranged!

The point is this: Music is needed. Maintenance is required. However, it must (at least) be balanced with authentic mission. Granted, reaching out to strangers is always more difficult—because it is more threatening. Besides, it is less satisfying to the ego than performing before our own crowd. Nevertheless, we must force ourselves to re-establish our priorities according to biblical standards. We must crash through the barrier of doing maintenance and become involved in authentic mission.

Second, we weave our webs selectively. We "web in" those who we feel will get us ahead. As for all others, we put them down ("You are below me on the social ladder"), put them on ("I'll never let you know the real me"), or put them off ("I'll keep you from having an authentic relationship with me").

What specific kinds of webbing do we prefer? There is elitism. We gravitate toward those we perceive to be important, persons who have influence in society, Y.A.V.I.S. people (i.e., *y*oung, *a*ctive, *v*erbal/*v*igorous, *i*ntelligent, *s*ociable). We think that our association with people "up there" can improve our own social standing.

Then there is nepotism, or limiting attention to relatives. Primary attention is given to kin relationship. There are Little League games for the children, weekend outings at the family cabin, and plenty of family reunions. We say to ourselves that God desires us to be concerned with our families, which is true. But he doesn't intend for us to neglect others.

Finally, there is cronyism. Put simply, this refers to pouring time and energy into involvement with the gang, the buddies, the crowd we run with. This small network is made up of people we closely associate with and deeply care about, that clique of persons that seems like family.

There is an overpowering temptation to gravitate to these three webs. Here we receive "strokes," feel secure, feel accepted and even flattered.

Unless we are biblically convicted and prayerfully cultivated, we do not involve ourselves with unpredictable, risky, low-status outsiders. Too much can go wrong with such associations. But we *must*. God commands it. He expects it, even though it may seem difficult and unpleasant.

But in setting out to weave webs of love, what should be kept in mind? What are some suggestions that can assist us?

Proceeding with Confidence

To begin with, it is imperative that we increasingly think in terms of "we" rather than "me." This is possible only if we counter a persistent, natural tendency to focus on ourselves.

The phrase *one another* is repeated no fewer than fifty-eight times in God's Word. Our perspective of concern must give priority to those with whom we share in Christ's body. Paul spells this out in his letter to the Philippian church: "Do nothing out of selfish ambition or vain conceit, but in humility consider others better than yourself" (2:3). Becoming even more specific, the apostle instructs, "Each of you should look not only to your own interests, but also to the interests of others" (v. 4). What is the basis of your advice, Paul? He answers, Because then "your attitude [will] be the same as that of Christ Jesus" (v. 5).

We must see ours as a corporate, not individual, identity. And if we do, we will "rejoice with those who rejoice [and] mourn with those who mourn" (Rom. 12:15). In short, we will "live in harmony with one another" (v. 16). We'll cooperate more than compete. Our Christian fellowship will continuously grow better. Or, as Charles R. Swindoll says, our church will become increasingly like grapes and decreasingly like marbles:

> Every congregation . . . can choose to be a bag of marbles, single units that don't affect each other except in collision. Or . . . a bag of grapes. The juices begin to mingle, and there is no way to extricate yourselves if you tried. Each is part of all. Part of the fragrance . . . [and] sometimes we 'grapes' really bleed and hurt."[7]

Second, we must prayerfully take the necessary measures to not allow conflicts to grow. At times the web of love wears thin and becomes frayed. It must be repaired immediately. If left unattended, small misunderstandings can quickly lead to conflict and alienation so that the entire body is adversely affected.

Jesus provides helpful advice: "Settle matters quickly with your adversary. . . . Do it while you are still with him on the way" (Matt. 5:25). Similarly, Paul states, ". . . do not let the sun go down while you are still angry, [for in so doing you] give the devil a foothold" (Eph. 4:26–27).

Every golfer knows that divots (pieces of sod skinned off the fairway) must be replaced immediately. Then they will take root and once again become part of the sod. But if they are allowed to dry out and wither in the sun, they cannot be replanted. An ugly scar is left. The analogy is obvious. Relationships taken care of quickly have a much better chance of healing without scars.

The first two suggestions mainly relate to love webs

7. Charles R. Swindoll, *Dropping Your Guard: The Value of Open Relationships* (Waco: Word, 1983), p. 178.

within the Christian fellowship. What about people who aren't a part, who display an interest in the Christian life, but have not been fully identified with the body? The final suggestion focuses on such persons.

As excellent Christians, we must give primary attention to those who have not been fully incorporated into the church fellowship. This is as difficult as it is necessary. Our lives become tightly interwoven with Christians we have known for some time.[8] As a result, we become oblivious to newcomers or marginally involved persons. Our ignoring them makes them feel even more estranged.

Something else contributes to the wearing of such blinders. Martin Marty refers to it as the bigotry-brotherhood paradox. In simple words it means the higher the morale of our group, the more likely it is that we will construct thick walls that exclude outsiders.[9] We feel so good about us that we become totally unconcerned about them.

Realizing these harmful tendencies, we must be on our guard. We must consciously plan to meaningfully interact with outsiders. One church with two thousand members asks members to greet four persons they don't know before greeting one they do know. Another church has newcomers go out to dinner with members. Creative plans abound and are working. The specific plan is not as im-

8. Church-growth experts have stated that it takes an average of two years for a new Christian to become fully incorporated/assimilated into a church. In so doing, he separates himself from the "old crowd" (see 2 Cor. 5:17). Howard Snyder is quoted as saying that the church must constantly win new people to Christ. These persons still have linkage with the "world" and are able to relate to other people who are not Christians. To have a preponderance of second-, third-, and fourth-generation Christians is to risk having broken contact with the unconverted.

9. Marty's term is elsewhere described thusly: "As we emphasize in-group unity, brotherhood, and oneness, we increasingly reject those unlike our kind. As a result our walls are built taller and thicker, our righteousness is increasingly paraded, and this causes an even greater rejection by outsiders." Jon Johnston, *Will Evangelicalism Survive Its Own Popularity?* (Grand Rapids: Zondervan, 1980), p. 71.

portant as the fact that action is being taken and that outsiders are being welcomed and integrated into the church body.

Typically, we do far better in welcoming persons than in slowly, patiently incorporating them. Many are given the "red-carpet treatment" as a first-time visitor to church. We pin a flower on their lapel and introduce them to the congregation. But then comes the letdown as people gravitate back to the cliques and ignore the outsider. We must realize that the welcome is only the beginning. As Paul declared, we must "become all things . . . so that by all possible means [we] might save some . . . for the sake of the gospel" (1 Cor. 9:22–23).

First, persons must be incorporated socially until they feel a sense of belonging and social comfort. This process follows a definite ten-step process. (See Figure 2.) In addition, the same individuals must be assimilated psychologically until there is a mutual trust between themselves and the church members. This can be thought of as taking place in eight steps. We must not be contented or rest until all persons in the body become fully incorporated and assimilated into the fellowship. To settle for less is to satisfy ourselves with something less than a New Testament church.

Well Worth the Effort

At least once a year our church has an open house and a special service for the parents of our day-school children. It is a relaxed, fun evening for everyone as we see the little ones perform in an uninhibited manner.

The teacher of our adult Sunday-school class foresaw an opportunity for us to become acquainted with our visitors. He made a strong appeal for all church members to be present and to be outgoing and friendly to the parents. So the church arranged to have light refreshments after the service.

FIGURE 2 **Incorporation/Assimilation Scale***

Incorporation (Social)		
	−10	Knows nothing of a particular church
	−9	Aware of church but knows no one in the church
	−8	Knows someone in the church
	−7	Has a personal friend in the church
	−6	Has two or more friends in the church
	−5	Has been involved in a social event related to the church
	−4	Has visited the church
	−3	Is involved in a church activity, for example, Bible study, recreational group
	−2	Attends church frequently
	−1	Familiarity with setting and worship style
	0	Feels sense of belonging and social comfort
	+1	Conversion
	+2	Regular attendance
	+3	Baptism
Assimilation (Psychological)	+4	Developing friendships
	+5	Church membership
	+6	Sanctification
	+7	Accepts responsibility
	+8	Trusted by membership

*From Win Arn and Charles Arn, *The Master's Plan for Making Disciples*, ed. Bill M. Sullivan (Kansas City, Mo.: Nazarene Publishing House, 1984), p. 44. Used by permission of James F. Engel.

Well, the time came for "us" to intermingle with "them." Unfortunately, few even bothered to show up. And those who did grouped together in a circle, totally excluding those for whom we had met.

It was frustrating, as you can imagine. Although the few of us who came managed to speak to all the visitors, we had little time to meaningfully interact, except with one couple that remained for a longer period of time.

These people were pleasant but thoroughly lonely, having just moved to California from the east. They complimented the church for its day-care facilities and began asking about the church. We invited them to attend. They immediately responded. The next Sunday they were there, along with several other families we had managed to invite.

The new couple began attending our Sunday-school class faithfully. Then a progression followed. They became involved in discussing the lesson, made friends with the other couples, accepted Christ as their Savior, and were elected officers for the class. The gentleman became the class president, a position he held for several years.

Our hearts were gladdened to see the couple attend every Sunday morning, both Sunday school and the morning worship service. However, few in the latter setting bothered to become acquainted with the "outsiders." It became embarrassing to continuously reintroduce them to the members for months and even years. Even so, the new couple kept coming. Gradually they became more involved: teaching Sunday school, supervising the nursery, and serving on the church board.

Now they are fully incorporated and assimilated into our fellowship. The small efforts we exerted on day-school evening paid rich dividends. Two beautiful persons were born into the kingdom of God and grew in Christian maturity. The church has accepted them in its web of love. May this scene be repeated scores of times in our congregation, as well as throughout all of Christendom!

10

Refusing to Cry "Uncle"

Do you remember B.D.A.C. (before the days of air conditioning)? I do. On a sweltering mid-August afternoon, we would open a window or eat an ice-cold popsicle. If the setting were Sunday church, we would fan ourselves. The local funeral home always provided an ample supply of fans, the kind made of cardboard. On one side was a picture of Jesus or a country church and on the other was an advertisement, such as, "Williams Funeral Home: The place with the convenient lay-away plan."

The point is this: We did survive, in spite of the odds. We literally didn't know what we were missing.

Today everything is different. Having the air conditioner malfunction is tantamount to having a three-alarm fire. It is a bona fide emergency. Next to food and water, it is a basic need for survival!

Why the change? It's simple. Our bodies have adapted to a new set of requirements. What once seemed uncom-

137

fortable seems torturous today. No longer does it seem "right" to endure high temperatures, even while eating ice cream.

In the same manner in which we adapt physically, we adapt morally to changing circumstances. Because of strong cultural influences, what once seemed right seems wrong and vice versa. We're swept along by the stream of social conformity, and the current is swift.

The key question is: Does God change as we change? Are his standards continuously adjusted to our own mindset and actions so that rightness and goodness are based on our unique situation?[1] Not at all.

We serve a God described by the writer of Hebrews as "the same yesterday and today and forever" (13:8). Our consistent God demands consistent obedience to his timeless commandments that he has recorded in his ageless Word. If there is adapting to be done, we must return to his changeless truths. He need not, as many seem to believe, adjust to the compromising pathways we have chosen.

As Christians who are deepening in biblical excellence, we will accept this important truth and live our lives accordingly. Furthermore, we'll be alert to the fact that we can be easily deceived by the perverted influences of our own culture. For, as Proverbs 16:25 warns, "There is a way that seems right to a man, but in the end it leads to death."

This means that we must have convictions and hold to them. Our convictions are our roots that connect us with the Source. Without them, we are little more than what Elton Trueblood terms "cutflower" Christians—shallow, frail, short-lived.

Mercedes-Benz ran an advertisement which stated, "Ex-

---

1. Situation ethics, a philosophical and religious viewpoint articulated by Joseph Fletcher, maintains an absence of objective standards. According to this belief, each situation demands its own response in accordance with the ethic of love. So, for example, if you subjectively deem it "loving" to commit adultery with your neighbor's wife, that is the best course of action.

cellence begins with how high you set your standards."
The same is true with Christian excellence. We must in-
ternalize and live according to God's lofty standards—but
with his faithful guidance and strength. Then our growth
in him is assured. Our spiritual roots tap into his inexhaustible supply.

Notice that I said "live according to his standards."
Many, like the Pharisees of old, rigidly maintain convictions that are not ordained by him. As Fritz Ridenour once
said, "They are so straight they make an arrow seem like
a snake." But it does them no good. In fact, it brings them
great harm, pushing them in the opposite direction of his
kind of excellence. What are some examples of such
convictions?

Standards That Stifle

First, some convictions are little more than superstitions. They are based on a notion, emotion, quirk, or
illusion.

Such fuzzy thinking is to be expected among pagans. In
600 B.C. the ancient Greeks were being defeated in battle.
A philosopher advised that the Areopagas be covered with
statues of all known gods. Then a flock of black and white
goats was allowed to roam on the same hill while the
Athenians carefully observed. Whenever a goat lingered in
front of a particular statue, the name of that god was written down and he was later worshiped. Stories involving
the use of such superstitious reasoning can be com-
pounded. Without knowledge of God's truth, such foolish
measures are frequently taken.

But as Christians, we should know better. We need not
rely on oracles, wizardry, shamanism, or blind fate. Our
God is personal and reasonable. There is nothing mysterious about his commands, and they are as near to us as
his Word.

In his famous tract, "Plain Account of Christian Perfection," John Wesley offered seven warnings to sanctified Christians. The second one was: "Beware of . . . enthusiasm." In that day, "enthusiasm" meant what he termed "heated imagination." We know it as fanaticism. The father of Methodism went on to say that dreams, voices, impressions, visions, and revelations are not good sources for determining our standards. He declared, "They may be from God. They may be from nature. Or they may be, and often are, from the devil." It is far better to receive guidance from his voice in prayer and by reading his written Word.

Second, some convictions attract attention for a selfish ego. When our appearance, speech, or behavior is eccentric, we stand out in the crowd. We separate ourselves from the masses. In short, the focus is on us. The reaction can be felt embarrassment or often pride.

In his great chapter about love, Paul declares, "If I give all I possess to the poor and surrender my body to the flames, but have not love, I gain nothing" (1 Cor. 13:3). What could attract more attention than these "noble" acts of sacrifice? But even they, if motivated by selfishness rather than *agape* love, are to no avail.

We must have convictions and stand by them consistently, regardless of the reactions of others. We owe no explanation, for we have received our direction from the Maker of the universe. However, we must not maintain and manifest such convictions in order to showcase a self that is eager to be in the spotlight.

Third, some convictions are generated by an unwillingness to accept change. People deny the new by hiding behind traditional beliefs and conduct.

A few centuries ago the church rejected scientific advancement. Galileo, Copernicus, and de Perthes were branded heretics for suggesting alternative conclusions. Inventions were denounced. For example, Sir James Simpson declared chloroform to be "a decoy of Satan that blesses women [during childbirth], but in the end hardens them and robs God of the deep, earnest cries that should arise to him in time of trouble."

Today some of us also slide into a "conviction rut" in order to avoid facing change. We become closed to such things as alternative ways of disciplining our children, different ways of communicating with our neighbors, and contrasting methods of serving our God. We're in a rut, which one person defined as "a grave with both ends kicked out." We have our security and don't wish to alter our set course.

To accept such a mind-set is to thwart our growth and to bring about an inevitable, traumatic collision with reality. We must not allow our standards to be used as vehicles of escape.

Finally, some convictions are exclusively negative. These convictions are perceived as sheer duty that we regard with distaste, do with reluctance, and later resent.

Augustine declared that the goal of all religion should be to enjoy God, not to chafe under the cloud of a rigid, negative ritualism. Why? If we are rigidly ritualistic, we picture God as a stern taskmaster rather than a Being of infinite love and excellence.[2]

Our convictions must liberate rather than imprison. They should resemble the tightness of a violin string, which provides the musician with freedom of movement and versatility of sound.

Certainly we must avoid self-defeating and God-dishonoring convictions. But the biggest problem does not lie in possessing the wrong variety of convictions nor even in having corrupt motives that underlie such standards. Rather, it is a severe erosion of any convictions.

---

2. Dean Kelley differentiates between stricture and stringency. The former is "systematically imposed by leadership." Such enforced norms lead to low morale. On the other hand, stringency occurs "spontaneously among the adherents." In contrast to stricture, stringency yields high morale. Dean M. Kelley, *Why Conservative Churches Are Growing: A Study in Sociology of Religion* (New York: Harper and Row, 1972), pp. 109–11.

The Drift Toward the Precipice

A small animal was seen riding on a log just above Niagara Falls. While swimming in the still water he had no doubt climbed onto the floating piece of wood to rest. Soon it began to move, at first slowly and then more rapidly toward the falls. He had a choice. He could either quickly jump off and swim back or he could continue with his joy ride. He chose the latter. According to eyewitnesses, he reached the churning rapids just above the falls. It was too late to jump. He clutched the log. As he saw the tremendous drop approaching, his fur stood up and his eyes bulged. Some shrieks of terror were heard. Then there was silence as he tumbled through the air to his doom.

Many of us compromise our convictions in a similar manner. We begin with good intentions. Rather than being malicious, we're simply careless. Our fateful course typically follows these steps:

1. Refrain from compromise, but forget why. The reasons for our convictions fade, and we become confused or less certain.
2. Begin going against our convictions and feel guilty.
3. Continue compromising until we feel less and less guilty.
4. Become oblivious to the standards we once held so dear.[3]

In my own childhood, Sunday used to be a day of rest. After church we'd read good books (or be read to), sleep, engage in quiet conversation, sing around the piano. Sunday buying was totally unacceptable. We reasoned: Store clerks should rest too. It is God's day.

---

3. The "worldly squeeze" is a gradual but directional process. Sociologists of religion think of it as occuring in three stages: accommodation, toleration of cultural/societal values (legitimation); assimilation, cooperation with cultural/societal values (participation); and amalgamation, fusion with cultural/societal values (identification). Jon Johnston, *Will Evangelicalism Survive Its Own Popularity?* (Grand Rapids: Zondervan: 1980), p. 36.

Then I "jumped on my log" to begin my drift toward compromise. As an "I'm-ready-to-begin-thinking-for-myself" teen-ager, I began to assert my independence. The plan was clever. I would pay the store clerks on Saturday for everything I'd be coming to get on Sunday. Then I could get around the Sunday-buying standard while technically not getting into trouble with my conscientious parents. The latter reluctantly went along with this practice, and I boasted about my ingenious scheme to everyone. By using brainpower, I had managed to sidestep the oppressive "Sunday-is-a-day-of-rest" routine. But, what is more significant, the drift had begun.

Today, Sunday buying is commonplace for me. It began with restricting purchases to "essentials." But now, everything desired is considered essential. And I don't even feel guilty. Perhaps I should.

We all have a strong temptation to climb onto the logs of compromise. The drift begins. We justify ourselves by claiming that we're being liberated. We're breaking out of the constraining fetters of legalism. Standards held in a previous time, when we were less enlightened, were foolish. In fact, we get a little embarrassed when we even think about them.

Granted, we must mature as the times change. What is considered worldliness in one era is not in another. As we grow in grace, God does help us to be more discerning. We know all that. But the temptation to drift is always present—especially with second-, third-, and fourth-generation Christians who have received their convictions secondhand. And, for some strange reason, all drifting that I know of is in the direction of becoming more liberal. What was previously considered wrong is now considered right—instead of the other way around. This fact concerns me greatly!

What does God's Word have to say about our convictions? Let's explore.

The Bible's Perspectives about Convictions

God's Word addresses the subject of this chapter directly. We know that the excellent Christian is commanded to obey, and to obey completely. As Samuel told disobedient King Saul, "To obey is better than sacrifice ..." (1 Sam. 15:22). What are we to obey? The commandments that are contained in the Bible.

What does obedience to his Word have to do with biblical excellence? Everything. Jesus tells us that our obedience is God's measuring stick for determining how much we really love him. You will recall that love and godly excellence are the same. John's Gospel recorded these words of our Master: "If you obey my commands, you will remain in my love, just as I have obeyed my Father's commands and remain in his love" (15:10). That is plain enough. God's directives to us must be obeyed. In fudging on them, we only wreak havoc for ourselves.

Biblical instruction approaches the subject of convictions from two perspectives: one negative and the other positive. One is focused on avoidance and the other is directed toward the dividend of such avoidance. But it should be remembered that they are opposite sides of the same coin.

We are told to reject the subtle temptation to become worldly. John 15:19 tells us that we "do not belong to the world." Romans 12:2 instructs us to "not conform any longer to the pattern of this world." James 1:27 warns us "to keep [ourselves] from being polluted by the world." Then, in 4:4 he declares, "Friendship with the world is hatred toward God." Perhaps the strongest verse of all is 1 John 2:15: "Do not love the world or anything in the world. If anyone loves the world, the love of the Father is not in him."[4]

4. L. A. King, "Where 'the World' Hangs Out," *Eternity*, November 1981, pp. 25–27.

In simple language, what does it mean to be worldly? It is to be worldlike—to think, feel, believe, act, and live like those whose lives are not under the lordship of Christ. It is an attitude of the heart.

Fritz Ridenour presents a helpful analogy. In his graphic words: "The old cliche compares Christians with ships and the secular world with water. The idea is that ships are to sail through the water, but water isn't supposed to get into the ships. . . .[God] is on the bridge shouting, 'Man the pumps!' "

But there is another side to this coin. Our motivation to consistently hold onto our convictions must be based on more than fear of disobedience. We must maintain our principles in order to enter into the abundant life that he has provided for us (see John 10:10) so that we might possess a full measure of his grace and reach our God-given potential.

What does it mean to live the abundant life? Revelation 3:15–16 tells us that we will keep our spirits and commitment at the boiling point. Lukewarmness will vanish. Paul, in his Second Letter to the Corinthians, promises that our heavenly Father will "always [cause] us to triumph in Christ" (2:14a, KJV). He adds, "Through us [he] spreads everywhere the fragrance of the knowledge of him. For we are to God the aroma of Christ among those who are being saved and those who are perishing" (2:14b–15).

Is there anything else? The apostle promises that "God richly provides us with everything for our enjoyment" (1 Tim. 6:17).

All of this and enjoyment too! What more could the world hope to offer?

Realizing the overwhelming dividends of obedience to God, we see our convictions and standards in a positive light. Rather than constraints, they are liberators. Rather than spirit-dampers, they are the very springboards that vault us to genuine fun and enjoyment. It is with good reason that author Jess Moody declares, "Fun was one of the chief characteristics of the apostolic church. 'Hilarious' was a New Testament adjective used to describe the saints."[5]

It is little wonder that Christians growing in excellence cease thinking in terms of what commandments they can sidestep. Instead, their line of reasoning is exactly the opposite. They ask, What more can I do, say, and be to reflect godliness and the abundant life? They do not seek to prove anything or earn God's favor. Rather, with cups overflowing, they yearn to nestle closer to the One they love most and to reflect his purity and power to the lost world.

In contrast to those motivated to compromise, Christians deepening in love "drift" in the direction of tightening up, getting rid of excess worldly baggage, even going a little overboard in sacrifice, as Mary did when Jesus came to visit. You'll recall that she poured perfume, her love gift, over her Lord's feet (John 12:3). It was pure nard, and one full pint, costing a year's wages. She definitely went overboard. But so did her Savior—for her, for all of us!

We draw strength and direction from God's Word on this critical issue. Convictions count with him. We must have the right kind, and stick by them come what may. But he promises to guide.

What practical suggestions might be offered to those of us who desire to develop a principled life?

Unbending Knees

Like Shadrach, Meshach, Abednego, and Daniel, who refused to bow down before King Nebuchadnezzar's golden image in ancient Babylon, we must keep stiff knees before the gods of compromise in our day (see Dan. 3). God expects us to stand tall in purity and expectancy. In resolv-

5. Jess Moody, *A Drink at Joel's Place* (Waco: Word, 1967), p. 19.

ing to not bow, the following suggestions could prove to be helpful.

First, we must be certain that our security is in God rather than in the reactions of men. Paul tells us to "serve wholeheartedly, as if [we] were serving the Lord, not men, because [we] know that the Lord will reward everyone for whatever good he does . . ." (Eph. 6:7).

As pilgrims in a foreign land, we can expect adverse reactions from those serving the spirit of the world. We cut across the grain of their basic nature. We rub them the wrong way.

Success, in the eyes of this world, means conforming to its pattern. This pattern Watchman Nee describes as the "mind behind the system," in short, the satanic principle which governs our planet (see Eph. 2:2).[6]

But when we strive for God's kind of excellence, an attainable standard rather than an elusive goal like success, he calls the shots. We have a heavenly Quarterback. What he tells us we do, knowing that his way will lead us to eternal victory—no matter how heated the "game of life" becomes.

The point is simple: We cannot please the world and God at the same time. In his high-priestly prayer to the Father, Jesus said that his disciples were hated by the world. Why? "For they are not of the world any more than I am of the world" (John 17:14).[7]

To overlook this important fact and to try to straddle the fence between God and Satan—in order to receive this world's acclaim—is a losing proposition. Short-term suffering might be avoided, but in a matter of time, the dis-

6. Watchman Nee, *Love Not the World* (Wheaton: Tyndale House, 1968), p. 38.

7. "The child of God will be involved in conflict with evil powers, and with Satan himself, if he earnestly undertakes to possess all that God has promised to him on this earth (cf. Ephesians 1:3, 6:10–18)." *Oxford NIV Scofield Study Bible,* "Introduction to Joshua" (New York: Oxford University Press, 1984), p. 225.

guise must be lifted. And both God and men charge betrayal.

As our Lord said, "No one can serve two masters" (Matt. 6:24). When we try, we can only gravitate toward the master of this world—Satan. But by choosing one Master, our heavenly Father, and considering his approval more than sufficient, life becomes fulfilling.

Second, we must be extremely careful in deciding what convictions to embrace. When we prayerfully and sincerely study the Scriptures—as did Paul's church at Berea (see Acts 17:11)—God's Spirit will guide us "into all truth" (John 16:13). Once his truth is lodged in our minds and heart, we are able to determine which things in our lives are in opposition to that truth.

What are such things? The mother of John Wesley sent a letter to her son, who was a student at Oxford University. It contained a stated rule of thumb concerning what kinds of convictions to have. Her words are wise: "Whatever weakens your reason, impairs the tenderness of your conscience, obscures your sense of God, or takes off the relish of spiritual things, whatever increases the authority of your body over your mind, that thing for you is sin."[8]

May we avoid all such things that dull the keen edge of our Christian experience and testimony. For to so indulge is, of certainty, to be willfully disobedient to the One who loves us so.

Finally, we must always remember that while biblical principles are general, convictions are personal. Convictions flesh out God's eternal principles in our individual lives so that his will is adapted to our unique situations and circumstances. This implies that we all have a tailor-made mission to fulfull with God's continuous direction.

Weaker Christians are known to have one strong tendency: being much harder on others than themselves. They

8. A. F. Harper, "Wisdom and Appetite," *The Enduring Word Adult Teacher: Great Topics of Wisdom Literature* (Kansas City, Mo.: Nazarene, 1984), pp. 34, 36.

castigate, condemn, judge. Psychologists term this projection, the practice of seeing our own weaknesses in others and criticizing the same harshly.

Christians growing in excellence become increasingly less judgmental of others and harder on themselves. They understand why Jesus sounded such a definite warning against all judging. The Master declared, "Do not judge, or you too will be judged" (Matt. 7:1). Just how are we judged by judging? Jesus continued, "For in the same way you judge others, you will be judged [by God], and with the measure you use, it will be measured to you" (v. 2). As our standards for others go up, God's expectation of us rises. That's plenty of incentive to put all measuring sticks away at once.

Nevertheless, we must bear down on our own commitment. As Canon H. P. Liddon once said, I must have a "heart of iron to myself [i.e., demanding], a heart of flesh to my neighbor [i.e., accepting], and a heart of fire [i.e., commitment] to my God."[9] By making certain that we are being true to the convictions he has given us, we become the best possible witness to the "unenlightened" and unsaved.

Jesus was such a model, and he attracted so many during his sojourn on earth. That's why those people found themselves spontaneously asking him, "What must I do to be saved?" And he told them. And they were.

Some Are Persecuted

Convictions—the kind that really set us apart from others—can make us feel more than a little uncomfortable. If we're not careful, we can begin feeling sorry for ourselves. Whenever I am tempted to do that, I often think of those whose faith costs them dearly in East Germany.

9. Canon H. P. Liddon, quoted in an editorial by William McCumber, *Herald of Holiness*, 1 September 1982, p. 16.

My wife and I accompanied a group of university students to this oppressive country where few smile. All colors seem drab. Freedoms that we take for granted are absent.

One of our students was granted permission to visit with an uncle. His visit lasted several hours. Upon his return, I couldn't help noticing that he was visibly shaken. In fact, he was crying as he told of what his relative had conveyed.

A Christian, the student asked the members of his uncle's family whether they were Christians. They responded by telling of the kind of persecution all believers must endure: loss of opportunity to attend college; loss of membership in the official Youth Corps, which means loss of job; continuous surveillance and harassment such as removing your telephone and censoring your mail. The list continued.

Then came the naive question: "But what if you would live a secret Christian life? What if your faith in Christ would go undetected?" It was explained that the government has ways of detecting true Christians. For one thing, Youth Corp meetings are scheduled during church times and attendance is compulsory. The uncle continued, "And even if you stay away from church—or refrain from verbally sharing your faith—they would still know if you're a true Christian." How? "It is obvious to them that you are living a different kind of life from that of others."

With such cold, calculated oppression, are there East Germans who live the Christian life? Many. And the numbers are growing. As "brands plucked from the burning," there are the courageous ones refusing to cry "uncle" to Satan and defying the threatening ultimatums of their government.

Just a few thoughts about their plight are enough to motivate me to hold fast to my convictions. Their steadfastness strengthens my own. May it strengthen yours.

We cannot without God, but God will not without us.
—Anonymous

Die when I may, I want it said of me that I plucked a weed and planted a flower wherever I thought a flower would grow. —Abraham Lincoln

The greatest asset is to have a liability; the greatest liability is to have no liability. —Louis Mann

The world is filled with willing people: Some willing to work, and the rest willing to let them. —Robert Frost

11

We Are All Gifted

It's an oft-repeated adage: Spiritual gifts—use them or lose them. My wife and I have attempted to use our talents in the work of God's Kingdom, but separately until last Christmas.

Our church asked us to be conarrators for the beautiful cantata "He Started the Whole World Singing." We were elated, for it was an opportunity to perform at our favorite church before our favorite people. Best of all, we'd be doing it together, using our God-given vocal talents.

We rushed out to purchase matching outfits. Then the rehearsals began. They were arduous, but necessary for the kind of perfection we planned to attain. Before long, the music and narration flowed together. This was bound to be an experience long remembered!

The big night arrived. Every seat was filled early. The decorations were immaculate. As anticipation soared, the choir filed in. My wife and I took our places behind the microphones. The dramatic prelude began. Everything went without a hitch. There was a standing ovation which seemed to never end. Did we ever feel fulfilled *together*!

The people demanded an encore performance a week later. They wanted to hear the concert again and to invite their friends to share in the experience. How could we turn them down?

My wife checked our calendar and noticed that some good friends from Illinois would be visiting on the day of our repeat performance. They had never been in our home or church before. It was perfect timing. We would treat them to the evening of their lives. After all, we should narrate even better the second time.

Preparation once again took place. Clothes were readied. Lines were rehearsed. Then our company arrived, and we sat down to dinner. It wasn't long before the conversation drifted toward our church and the upcoming event. Our guests were overjoyed to know that they would be seeing us perform. In addition to the Rose Bowl game, this would be a highlight of their trip.

Then the telephone rang. The voice on the other end was abrupt. The response was one of shock. "We have what?! . . . Been replaced? Oh, replaced." No reason was given. Our lines had simply been given to someone else. And what an uncomfortable time we had breaking the news to our bewildered friends. They just looked at us. Then we all started laughing. Before long, everything was in perspective again. We concluded that it was another of life's curve balls. And we had struck out swinging.

We've all had high hopes of serving in an important capacity, only to be told, "Sorry, we've had a change of plans. You won't be needed after all." Intense disappointment followed, along with the temptation to refuse when asked again. Some of us have muttered to ourselves, "If this is the way people are treated, no wonder they hesitate to become involved. Few enjoy being a masochist!"

The truth is that many of us do resist using our God-given spiritual gifts for his glory. In biblical parlance, we put our "candle . . . under a bushel" (Matt. 5:15, KJV). Often this is not our preference. As we observe the overworked, overexposed minority do everything, we find ourselves wishing that we could have a part, for God's kingdom and for ourselves. Why are our aspirations short-circuited? Let's examine some possible reasons.

Roadblocks and Detour Signs

The first two reasons focus on why some of us have never started to utilize our natural endowments in service to God. They can be perceived as roadblocks.

First, many of us feel inferior. As a result, we develop an intense shyness and timidity. We think, "When you're as bad as I am, you don't take risks. Instead, I must hide. Not behind trees, like I did when I was a child, but behind excuses and in the shadows of those who are more qualified."

Those of us who are multitalented have less temptation to withdraw into passivity. When one gift fails, another can be pulled out of the bag. There's always a support sytem. But when we possess only one talent—the minimum allotment for every human being created by God— there is a tendency for us to bury it.

Jesus supports this conclusion in his parable of the talents. The person given five talents went at once and gained five more, as did the one with two talents. "But the man who had received the one talent went off, dug a whole in the ground and hid his . . ." (Matt. 25:18). The ones with hefty endowments increased them and flaunted their gain. But the poor fellow who was given one gift hid it. He did not just hide it, but he buried it in the ground. The thought of having to later explain his poor stewardship no doubt made him want to climb into the same hole!

The world expresses this principle graphically. "Them that has gets." "When you're hot, you're hot." "It takes

money to make money." "When you've got it, flaunt it."
This implies, "When you don't have it, don't look to get
it." "When you're not hot, you're cold." "When you don't
have money, forget trying to make it." "When you don't
have it, hide it."

Many sociologists believe that the overpowering temptation for the single-gifted person to hide it is intensified
in a large church. It is easy to be anonymous. Also, it
seems foolish to compete against superior talent. The con-
ception (or misconception) is: With this many people, there
must be enough talented people to fill all areas of responsibility. Ministers of large churches would argue with this
conclusion, but it is a pervasive belief nevertheless and
has some justification.[1]

Second, some of us allow time to sneak up. We are
convinced of the importance of using our talents for God.
We're not timid. We intend to get involved—some day.
But we procrastinate. And, as one writer put it, "Procrastination is the thief of time."

All of life can legitimately be perceived as a race against
the clock. Someone described middle age as "that period
of life when we try to use up what Mother Nature has
given us, before Father Time takes it away."

Unfortunately, we often fail to comprehend the brevity
of life. James describes man as "a mist that appears for a
little while and then vanishes" (James 4:14b). But regardless of our illusions, earthly existence is finite. There is
an end as well as beginning. The average man lives but
seventy-four years.[2] That is approximately 888 months,

---

1. A complete treatise about the small church in relationship to super
church is presented in *The Smaller Church in a Super Church Era*, ed. Jon
Johnston and Bill M. Sullivan (Kansas City, Mo.: Beacon Hill, 1983). Special
mention of the participation factor in the small church is on pp. 31–32, as
well as in other locations.

2. Average life expectancy (A.L.E.) has varied throughout human history.
For the ancient Romans it was thirty-eight years. For Native Americans today,
it is forty-four years. It should be noted that the variance is mostly due to
infant mortality. For example, in Ecuador, 60 percent of all children die before
age five. That, of course, lowers the overall A.L.E. When Americans point with

3,848 weeks, 27,010 days, 648,240 hours, 38,894,400 minutes and 2,022,508,800 heartbeats. One writer focuses on life's brief stages:

> Tender teens,
> Teachable twenties,
> Tireless thirties,
> Fiery forties,
> Forceful fifties,
> Sacred sixties,
> Sinking seventies,
> Aching eighties,
> Shortening breath,
> Death,
> The sod,
> And God.

My college roommate, Mike, had a sign on his desk. I thought about it often, and even memorized the words:

> But one life,
> t'will soon be past.
> Only what's done for Christ
> will last.

In my world travels, I have observed the ruins of man's greatest achievements: the Jerusalem temple, the Egyptian pyramids, the Temple of Diana in Ephesus, the Great Wall of China. All that remains are crumbling, flaking rocks. But the words of Mike's poem penetrated my mind most deeply when, last summer, I visited Caesarea in Israel. It was King Herod's crowning glory—the same Herod who killed Bethlehem's male babies, trying to murder baby Jesus.

pride to the fact that the A.L.E. for males is seventy-four years, it must be remembered that this figure differs little from the one mentioned in Psalm 90:10: "The length of our days is seventy years—or eighty, if we have the strength; yet their span is but trouble and sorrow, for they quickly pass, and we fly away." In short, the A.L.E. has varied little in the course of history. People unencumbered by disease or war seem to live a life that averages the "threescore years and ten" (KJV) that is mentioned by the psalmist.

The year was 12 B.C. The haughty king invited the world to Caesarea for the Olympic Games. People came from everywhere to the golden city of enchantment. The featured event was horse racing, held in the city's extravagant Hippodrome.

After providing this historical background, our guide stopped the bus beside a huge cornfield with banked sides. Some Arab farmers toiled in the hot sun. Beside the road was a columned arch. It was all that remained of Herod's famous Hippodrome, once the envy of the ancient world. Today, it is only a tourist site.

> Only what's done for Christ
> will last.

Life is short. There is no time to waste. Yet we do, and with the best of intentions. Like the rich man in God's Word, we keep building our own barns and saying to ourselves, "You have plenty of good things laid up for many years. Take life easy; eat, drink and be merry" (see Luke 12:16–21). There is no need to become involved in God's work today. There's always tomorrow.

But these are roadblocks that keep people from ever getting involved. What about those of us who are attempting to use our God-given talents for his work? What are some detours that throw us off track, send us in the wrong direction, or put us on a road where we can only spin our wheels?

First, it is quite possible to be replaced, even when we feel deeply that we are fulfilled and in the center of God's will.

Sometimes we're forced to bow out, or at least to take a position of less recognized importance. Someone thought to be more talented comes along. No longer is our advice or participation requested. We're shelved.

Second, often we fall prey to overexposure and overinvolvement. We try to do too much, for ego sake or because others refuse to pick up the torch of responsibility.

As a result we feel taken for granted by the apathetic

and overlooked by those who bestow credit. Oh, we keep going, but what we once did joyfully becomes burdensome. Rather than anticipating, we dread. An acute case of burnout sets in. We go through the motions, without a real sense of mission.

In the secular world, this is a day of specialization. The latest Gallup Poll lists the multitude of job titles held by Americans. To read some is to smile. Can you imagine having these listed on your job resume: Teabag Stringer, Tombstone Polisher, or Chicken Sexer (person who examines the underside of baby chicks to determine whether they are male or female). During summers of her college years, my wife held such illustrious employment positions as Pitter (removing seeds from peaches) and Huller (separating almond shells from the outer hulls). Truly, this is a day of specialization. The advantage is that one person doesn't have to be an expert in all areas. That means a lot when everything is so complicated and seems to be getting more so.

It is unfortunate that what we have learned in the marketplace we often fail to apply to the church. God made us all specialists by granting us specific spiritual gifts. To attempt to do everything, including what others should (and could) be doing is to eliminate the possibility of reaching our God-intended potential. Our heavenly Father does not want us to drive ourselves to burnout, which can only render us useless. This detour must be avoided at all costs!

What wise instruction does God's holy Word give us about the use of our spiritual gifts?

Using Our Loaves and Fishes

It was time for the Passover feast. But the crowds, on their way to Jerusalem, were intent on seeing and hearing the Man who was performing miracles. Five thousand of them followed him to the hillside overlooking the Sea of Galilee. As he spoke they were mesmerized. They lost track of time.

Jesus became concerned about their need for bodily nourishment and shared that concern with some of the disciples. Philip threw up his hands in frustration: "Eight months' wages would not buy enough bread for each one to have a bite!" (John 6:7). But Andrew located a small boy with five small barley loaves and two small fish. After revealing this to the Lord, he sadly declared, "But how far will they go among so many?" (v. 9).

Christ saw an opportunity for a miracle as well as an important spiritual object lesson. After he said grace, the food was multiplied. All five thousand were fed and twelve "doggie bags" full of leftovers were collected. What was the lesson? The One who said, "Anyone who will not receive the kingdom of God like a little child will never enter it" (Mark 10:15) chose to use the gift of a powerless lad. The bearer of the gift was lowly, without power and status. He was simply an intrigued youthful bystander. In addition, the gift that he bore was insignificant in the eyes of the world. His loaves were probably mashed and stale. And we all know what happens to fish that has been exposed to the hot sun.

The only component of value in this entire scenario was the boy's willingness to present his gift to the Master. He offered all he had. That is what God wants of us. As John D. Rockefeller said at the dedication of the United Nations Building in New York City, "We are stewards of all God gives us—and that for a little while." To begin with, it is necessary for us to lay our loaves and fishes at his feet—willingly, and even cheerfully. As Paul states, "Not reluctantly or under compulsion, for God loves a cheerful giver" (2 Cor. 9:7).

But in presenting our gifts to the Master, what does God's Word instruct us to keep in mind?

First, we all have a special and unique sphere of influence. There are people that only we can reach. Somehow we have earned their attention and trust. They listen to what we say, and do what we do. As a result, in the biblical perspective, they are our responsibilities.

Jesus talks about the "faithful and wise servant" who the master puts in charge of the other servants while he is on a trip (Matt. 24:45–51). Such a person is in charge of the household. In effect, Jesus is saying that we are all in charge of something. We all have a "household." The Greek term for "household," *oikonomia*, literally means "sphere of influence." We must accept our responsibility with the utmost seriousness. Our best gifts and talents must be conscientiously appropriated to the task at hand, for we are our Master's representative, operating under his authority and power. There must be no holding back, no laziness, no passing the buck. The One who enables us to effectively serve, generously providing us with spiritual gifts, expects us to fulfill our mission.

Second, the sharp distinction we have made between "minister" and "layman" must be revised according to biblical direction. We are all ministers within our circles of influence, be they on the job, at school, or at church.

Recently I read James L. Garlow's *Partners in Ministry*. It contains some rather startling statements: "Religion is too serious a business to be left to the clergy." Also: "If football is twenty-two men on the field who desperately need rest, and 60,000 in the stands who desperately need exercise," church can be described as "a few desperately weary clergy—being cheered on by many spectators who desperately need the essential exercise of ministry."

Garlow points out that the New Testament word for "layman" (*laos*) means "person of God." That's not something to be taken lightly. Peter, in his first epistle, lists five things every "person of God" is: a living stone (resting on the cornerstone, which is Jesus); a chosen person; a royal priest; a citizen of a holy nation; and one of God's very own persons (2:4–5, 9–10). In short, we are authentic ministers of the gospel![3]

Where does this leave our professional clergy? Are they

3. James L. Garlow, *Partners in Ministry: Laity and Pastors Working Together* (Kansas City, Mo.: Beacon Hill, 1981), pp. 11–22, 39.

still needed? Absolutely. Freed from having to motivate us to minister, they can become equippers, teaching and training us to be "work[men] who [aren't] ashamed and who correctly handle the word of truth" (2 Tim. 2:15). In addition, they can become "player-coaches" who take the lead in being as well as doing. Paul instructs Timothy: "Set an example for the believers in speech, in life, in love, in faith and in purity" (1 Tim. 4:12). In short, they are master shepherds who head a church full of shepherds in caring for God's lost sheep.

Finally, after recognizing our sphere(s) of influence and considering ourselves authentic ministers, we must begin to prayerfully minister in accordance with our spiritual gifts.

Some of us aren't sure which gifts we possess. To begin with, we should consult the lists of gifts in God's Word. Kenneth Kinghorn has summarized them (see Table 1).

TABLE 1*

Romans 12:6–8	1 Corinthians 12:4–11	1 Corinthians 12:28	Ephesians 4:11
Prophecy Teaching Serving Exhortation Giving Giving Aid Compassion	Prophecy	Prophecy Teaching	Prophecy Teaching
	Healing Working Miracles Tongues and Their Interpretation Wisdom Knowledge Faith Discernment	Healing Working Miracles Tongues and Their Interpretation	
		Apostleship Helps Administration	Apostleship
			Evangelism Shepherding

*From *Gifts of the Spirit* by Kenneth Kinghorn. Copyright © 1976 by Abingdon Press. Used by permission.

After becoming aware of the potential gifts, we must attempt to pinpoint our strong and weak areas. Refer to the Trenton Spiritual Gifts Analysis in Appendix A. This simple test can be of great assistance in determining those areas that we should be most intent on cultivating. Grade the test and read the specific scriptural references that apply to your highest scores (i.e., strongest gifts). Spend some time in prayer of intense commitment and for guidance as you proceed to develop and use your spiritual gifts. This exercise can be extremely rewarding.

Are there any suggestions that might prove helpful in pursuing this course? Perhaps there are.

A Needed Perspective

First, with God's help, we must chart a steady course as we use our spiritual gifts for him. This means directing our primary attention to our heavenly Father. He bestowed our talents in the first place. He helps us refine and effectively utilize those talents in his kingdom. He deserves all praise when others respond favorably to our display of spiritual gifts.

When we accept that everything is in his hands, we can rest patiently (i.e., be in a state of expectant readiness; see Ps. 37:7). When that occurs, life ceases to be a discord. Instead, there is harmony and rhythm, meaning and fulfillment. We are neither demolished by insult nor unduly inflated by compliment. We know we're dependent upon him.

Knowing this fact had a positive effect on Paul, who was persecuted. Acts 28:15b declares, "Paul thanked God and was encouraged." As one concert violinist kept his eyes riveted on his teacher in the balcony, so the apostle fixed his eyes on his Master (see Heb. 12:2). Paul's life became like a beautiful symphony. His course was steady. He was at peace.

Second, in being a faithful steward of our spiritual gifts, we must be more concerned with internal fulfillment than external applause. To receive his smile is to be rewarded. Or, as 2 Timothy 2:15 puts it, being "approved of God" is the ultimate.

Like secular excellence (see chap. 2), Christian excellence focuses on a standard rather than a goal. However, you will recall that the latter is a self-imposed measurement based on personal potential, whereas the former is what this world deems important and rewards with the only currency it possesses: power, privilege, and wealth. But as Christians, our standard is God's unchanging Word. In addition, it is to increasingly reach our potential for using our spiritual gifts for his glory. Unlike the world, our divine Paymaster rewards our growth process as well as our final product.

For us, it matters not who looks or who looks the other way. We do not depend on their fickle reactions for our satisfaction. Nor do we envy those who succeed. As the Psalmist says, we do "not fret when men succeed in their ways" (37:7b). Success that is derived from Christian excellence, received in gratitude, and reconsecrated to God is entirely commendable. Success outside this realm is not enviable because it is the only payoff its recipients will ever receive.

People are not our master. Nor are the trinkets they wave before our eyes as they attempt to lure us in their direction. Rather, we serve One who penetrates deeper than the external. He rewards the deepest recesses of our inner spirits with an indescribable joy.

This kind of joy Carl Lewis gave witness to before the international media. He unequivocally stated that his greatest satisfaction in life is his vibrant, personal relationship with Jesus. Standing beside this, his record-setting four gold medals pale in significance! He, like all of us who have embarked on the journey of Christian excellence, can anticipate that ultimate reward on the day of judgment when our Lord will address us by name and say, "Well done, thou good and faithful servant: thou hast been faithful over a few things, I will make thee ruler over many things: enter thou into the joy of thy lord" (Matt. 25:21, kjv).

Finally, as our spiritual gifts yield ever-increasing dividends, we must increase in generosity. As my father used to tell his parishioners, "We must give until it hurts, then give some more—until it quits hurting." As was emphasized in our Lord's reaction to the widow's mite (Luke 21:1–4), all giving to God must be sacrificial. He deserves, and desires, the best that we have.

It was a snowy Sunday morning, the day before a soldier was to go to war. He attended the morning worship service at his church. The offering plate was passed. Later, while counting the money, the ushers noticed a crumpled note. Scratched out in pencil were two simple words: One life. Rather than tossing in a few coins, the soldier had offered God all that he possessed.

We are asked to do the same. What does our divine Master require of us? Everything. Recall the story of the servant left in charge of his landlord's household (Matt. 24:45–51). The steward neither had nor made any claim to ownership. His task, like ours, was to conscientiously apply the best of his abilities to the responsibilities he had agreed to assume—undergirded by his master's complete blessing and authority.

As God increases our responsibility and prosperity, we must do more than say thanks and hoard. Our task is not barn-building and amassing a fortune. Rather, we must forever realize that we are given more in order to give more. Our tight fists must relax as we allow their contents to slip through our fingers and land on areas of severe need. These areas are close to the heart of God.

This Takes the Cake!

Stewardship is the business of all of us. We are all gifted by our loving Creator. Each gift given us, no matter how seemingly insignificant, is capable of being infinitely expanded. When gifts are expanded and appropriated, God is glorified!

My recently deceased mother-in-law was reared in a Kansas farm community as an orphan. She was always shy, choosing to stand behind people at a social gathering. Her feelings of inferiority were many and intense. She would cover her mouth when smiling, not allowing others to observe her facial expressions.

Although she was a committed Christian, she'd be the first to admit that she was not richly endowed with spiritual gifts. In fact, it took many years for her to discover one. But that one made all the difference in the world—even though it isn't listed (except by inference) on the official biblical list of gifts.

It began when, just for fun, she entered a local baking contest. To her amazement her entry, chocolate layer cake, captured the first-place ribbon. It was the first honor like this that she had ever received. Immediately she was invited to enter the winning recipe in the Butte County (California) Fair. Again she won. The recipe was featured in the *Best Cooks of the West: Butte County Cookbook.* All of her friends, and scores throughout the city, read about her winning entry. She became known as "that great cook" (a well-deserved title, as I can personally attest).

Mom began to take great comfort in what she perceived to be her one and only talent. It gave her some confidence in other areas of her life—but areas always related to baking. Then she began to use her spiritual gift for the Lord. A baking ministry was started. Cookies, cakes, and pies were made for convalescent homes throughout the town. That kept her busy, but extremely fulfilled.

God blessed her unique service to his kingdom. Before long, the recipients of her benevolence began telephoning. They shared their joys as well as their heartbreaks. And she listened. Others began attending her church—and kept attending.

Without a doubt, Mom's gift, when returned to God in humble obedience, was multiplied in its effects. She left us with a helpful, encouraging lesson: We're all truly gifted, even those of us who, by comparison with others, possess fewer of God's bestowments. As the song declares with certainty: "Little is much when God is in it!"

There are three things which cannot come back: the spent arrow, the spoken word, and the lost opportunity. —William Barclay

Any direction, just so it be forward. —Anonymous military general

The journey of a thousand miles begins with one step. —Chinese proverb

No problem is so awesome, so complicated, so fraught with danger that the average citizen can't run away from it. —Charlie Brown (*Peanuts* comic strip)

12

Daring to Act

During my years in seminary I knew him as a prolific scholar, captivating professor, intense ping-pong competitor, and absent-minded friend. This man was so absent-minded that the favorite student pastime was trading accounts of his unbelievable antics: mailing his wife's groceries, or walking home after forgetting that he had driven his car to town.

His life was a study in contrast. From a humble, even primitive, childhood home in the Ozarks, he ascended to (and excelled in) educational institutions of renown. He once wrote an autobiographical article, which he appropriately entitled "From the Ozarks to Oxford."

Perhaps the simple and impoverished roots caused his deep compassion for the needy. He spoke of that concern often. So did his colleagues. It was the trendy thing to do in the late 1960s.

But there was a difference when *he* spoke. A certain pathos in his voice betrayed a first-hand experience. The pain of destitution had been indelibly etched on his psyche. As a result, he manifested the depth of empathy that only direct involvement can provide.

His kind of empathy made him discontent with second-hand information. He yearned to once again feel the gnawing pangs of hunger, the extreme discomforts of crowded living conditions, to learn more about the plight of the have-nots, and even to identify with them in their misery. So he decided to act.

My compassionate professor put on ragged clothes, grew a shaggy beard, and set out for the ravaged, restless inner cities of America, not for a few token days, but for many long months. He limited himself to the junglelike survival tactics of his desperate neighbors: begging for meager handouts, sleeping in the rat-infested doorways of slum apartments, and competing for degrading jobs, only to repeatedly endure cold rejection.

Finally it was time to return to that "sophisticated jungle" we know as civilized, middle-class America. But he returned with renewed and expanded insight that was generously shared with, and deeply affected, students like myself. We received a wealth of valuable, first-hand information and along with it, an inescapable burden for the forgotten, powerless, and destitute of our land.

But even more impressive than the knowledge we gleaned and the captivating experiences he shared was his courage to act: to depart from his understanding family and follow his compelling heart to the scene of his great concern—the ghettos of our nation.

Like him, we must dare to act, to put ourselves on the line, to have enough courage to break the fetters of apathy and respond to our heartfelt convictions.

Our actions need not be as radical as his. God guides each of us to follow our own star. But the inescapable fact is that we all must act. We must assert ourselves in faith.

Withdrawal can lead only to loss of function, as any of us who have had a broken arm in a cast can attest.

This is not to minimize excellence of mind and intention. But, as we read in chapter 4, we must move on to excellence in loving deeds. In so doing we learn first-hand that our heavenly Father guides, empowers, and rewards those who lovingly assert themselves in his name.

Give Me This Mountain!

Most of us can recall from childhood Sunday-school lessons the story of the twelve Hebrew spies who scouted the land of Canaan (Num. 13–14). Although ten of them saw conquest as impossible, Caleb and Joshua said, in effect, "Let's go for it. With God by our side, we will conquer!" Their plea fell on deaf ears. Fear gripped the people and they even "talked about stoning" (14:10) these advocates of sheer suicide. Moses was influential enough to prevent that. But the Hebrews refused to act. Instead, they wandered aimlessly in the Sinai Desert for forty years.

By then Moses had died. Joshua had assumed leadership of the nation as God directed. The belated command was given, and God's people invaded Canaan. Cities were conquered, one by one. But all the nation was not purged of Canaanites. Stubborn pockets of guerrilla fighters remained, especially in the treacherous hill country.

Who would step forward with the necessary leadership skills and courage to drive them out? Caleb, the son of Jephunneh! Unlike the much younger spy of forty, he was now a white-haired senior citizen of eighty-five.

I can imagine the scene. Everyone's favorite grandfather enters the tent of his commander-in-chief, Joshua. Joshua says, "Good afternoon, Caleb, how are you feeling today? Is your rheumatism acting up again? Are you remembering to take your medicine? It's necessary, you know."

With a spark in his eye, the elderly gentleman replies,

"Forget about my aches and pains, Joshua, I have something to tell you. And I want you to listen carefully."

> I was forty years old when Moses . . . sent me from Kadesh Barnea to explore the land. And I brought him back a report according to my convictions, but my brothers who went up with me made the hearts of the people melt with fear. I, however, followed the LORD my God wholeheartedly. So on that day Moses swore to me, "The land on which your feet have walked will be your inheritance and that of your children forever, because you have followed the LORD my God wholeheartedly."
>
> Now then, just as the LORD promised, he has kept me alive for forty-five years since the time he said this to Moses, while Israel moved about in the desert. So here I am today, eighty-five years old! I am still as strong today as the day Moses sent me out; I'm just as vigorous to go out to battle now as I was then. Now give me this hill country ["Give me this mountain," KJV] that the LORD promised me that day. You yourself heard then that the Anakites were there and their cities were large and fortified, but, the Lord helping me, I will drive them out just as he said. [Josh. 14:7–12]

Caleb was saying, in effect, "I'm ready for action. It's time to take care of business. Let's go with God!"

If I had been Joshua, I might have put my arm around the old fellow and said, "Caleb, your spirit is commendable. Your attitude is a fine example. You certainly haven't lost your fight. But we must be reasonable. You're twenty years past retirement. Why not relax now? Go find a comfortable rocking chair, and hold your grandchildren on your lap. Let the rest of us take it from here on."

But Caleb was a person of action, old age or no old age. Joshua must have known this, for he granted his request. The area of (and surrounding) Hebron was given to Caleb to conquer (v. 13). Conquer he did—which is not unlike most persons of action.

The pertinent question is: Why do many of us who are younger and more able-bodied than Caleb hesitate to accept a soul-stretching challenge? Why are we, as Fritz Ridenour puts it, "about as swift as a speeding glacier" when it comes to pushing ahead to action? Let's examine some reasons.

Why Deeds Are Short-Circuited

There are almost as many reasons for nonaction as there are persons who avoid taking action. But perhaps the most conspicuous of these reasons can be discussed.

First, many of us would rather talk than act. We've heard the expression *talk is cheap,* and it is. Our verbiage can provide us with a convenient illusion of involvement.

We do a lot of talking on a university campus. Great quantities of information are imparted, discussed, and responded to on examinations. But there is little action. This fact prompted one of my colleagues to declare, "I often feel that my teaching is like filling a bathtub with facts. At test time, the student pulls the plug and all goes down the drain at once. And there's not even a 'ring of memory' left." In addition, students aren't given sufficient opportunity to act upon what they do retain.[1]

For many of us, talk is easy and action is hard. And because of this, inactivity reigns. We're affected by what the late author and missionary to India, E. Stanley Jones, termed "the paralysis of analysis."

Second, some of us possess a nonassertive tempera-

---

1. I have recently noticed some significant movement in academia to provide students with opportunities for action. For example, in-class experiments as well as out-of-class fieldwork illustrate abstract principles. My own university has instituted a tutorial program for juvenile offenders at Camp David Gonzales. The wards are taught math, English, and related courses on a one-to-one basis. Our students report that such action on their part yields increased self-confidence, more sensitivity to human need, greater understanding of the outside world, and expanded ability to conceptualize the connection between theory and reality.

ment. Whether it's because we were born that way, or became that way through conditioning, we find it more "natural" to avoid taking action.

It is important that we understand our basic temperament and pinpoint our strengths. As the Seven Sages advised, "Know thyself." A Greek physician, Hippocrates, outlined four temperament types which have been consistently referred to through the centuries. They are sanguine (happy, chatty, forgetful); choleric (leaders, drivers, dominating); melancholic (thinkers, perfectionists, sensitive); and phlegmatic (calm, easy-going, indecisive). Refer to Appendix B, which provides a more thorough explanation of the types and a simple test for determining one's temperament type.

Third, some of us avoid action because we realize that it involves risk. To do is to take a chance of something going wrong:

> To laugh is to risk appearing the fool.
> To weep is to risk appearing sentimental.
> To reach out for another is to risk involvement.
> To expose feelings is to risk exposing your true self.
> To place your . . . dreams before the crowd is to risk their loss.
> To love is to risk not being loved in return.
> To live is to risk dying.
> To hope is to risk despair.
> To try is to risk failure.[2]

The faint of heart, the unwilling of spirit, hesitate to take such risks. For them it is good enough to remain tucked away in the secure nest of inaction.

Fourth, some of us refrain from doing because we think that others will (or should). Someone jokingly defined a college president as a person "who looks at the dirtiest,

2. Seen in *Humanican,* an informal newsletter for Youth Agency Administration students at Pepperdine University, 28 January 1982, p. 2.

meanest job and tells his assistant to get it done at once." Passing the buck is easy to do, especially when we know that there are others who can or will take action. In social psychology, this principle is known as the bystander effect.[3]

Action-oriented persons are likely to assume responsibility, regardless of who might (or should) be involved. Completing tasks is primary in their estimation.

Finally, more than a few of us sense an inner need to be passive and await our destiny. We believe in fate. What's "written in the stars" is believed to be certain and inescapable.

Such a belief destroys ambition, and "can do" optimism is evaporated. The only thing left is to receive what fate has in store and to adjust accordingly. I heard an amusing story about a fatalist who tumbled down a flight of stairs. He got up, brushed himself off, and with a big smile said, "Well, I'm sure glad that's over." In other words, it was bound to happen; I just didn't know when. Now that the suspense is over, I can relax until the next blow of fate.

Without a doubt, this (or any) kind of fatalism can kill enthusiasm for action. What's the use? If all is predetermined, what difference can our efforts possibly make?

There are other defeating short-circuits to action: becoming sidetracked by trivial matters, expecting reward for everything done, or awaiting the right kind of leadership. The list is seemingly unending.

What does God's Word say about the necessity of taking action? Are there specific directives that we must seriously consider? Let's explore.

---

3. John M. Darley and Bibb Latane have studied the conditions under which people become willing to help one another. Their interest in the subject was generated by the Kitty Genovese story. She was murdered, although for one-half hour she screamed and cried for help while thirty-eight persons witnessed the event. No move was made to help her or even to call the police. The researchers found statistical support for the following principle: The more people that are present in an emergency, the less likely it is that any one of them will make a helpful action. Lawrence S. Wrightsman, *Social Psychology in the Seventies* (Monterey, Calif.: Brooks/Cole, 1972), p. 34.

The Christian Action Manual

The Bible can rightly be perceived as an inspired account of how God has acted on our behalf in history. He acted not because we earned or deserved it (see Eph. 2:8–9), but because of his unconditional, limitless, and excellent love.

When our hearts become saturated with the same love, we too will act. We will make a committed effort to spread his love through deeds and actions. We do this not to earn his favor (see Titus 3:5), but as an outgrowth and natural response of our love for him.

What does God's Word declare concerning action taking in the life of the Christian?

First, we are commanded to pray for godly action to take place. Without such action, God's kingdom will not expand on earth.

Curtis Mitchell has written an intriguing article which strongly suggests that our Lord never prayed directly for the eternal salvation of lost souls. In addition, Paul offered but one explicit prayer for the latter (Rom. 10:1). Certainly both cared deeply for the unsaved.[4] How, then, did they choose to pray?

Instead of praying for the harvest, our Lord chose to entreat God for the harvesters, the ones who would take action under the Father's power. In Matthew 9:37–38 we read: "Then he said to his disciples, 'The harvest is plentiful but the workers are few. Ask the Lord of the harvest, therefore, to send out workers into his harvest field.' "

Similarly, when Paul was imprisoned he penned a letter

---

4. In several instances, Christ and Paul prayed for the unsaved indirectly. Jesus instructed us to "pray for those who persecute you" (Matt. 5:44, NASB). The greatest benefit for such an unsaved persecutor would be his conversion. Similarly, Paul argued that prayers be offered "for kings and all those in authority, that we may live peaceful and quiet lives in all godliness and holiness" (1 Tim. 2:2). Behind his immediate objective is a more crucial one, that God "wants all men to be saved and to come to a knowledge of the truth" (2:4). Thus, prayer for unsaved government officials is implied. Curtis Mitchell, "Don't Pray for the Unsaved!" *Christianity Today*, 16 September 1983, p. 28.

that requested prayer not for his release from prison, but rather for his effectiveness in preaching the gospel. Ephesians 6:19–20a declares, "Pray also for me, that whenever I open my mouth, words may be given me so that I will fearlessly make known the mystery of the gospel, for which I am an ambassador in chains" (see also Col. 4:3). He requested that the believers pray for him as he proclaimed the message of salvation.

Why didn't he request prayer for his fellow prisoners, mentioning them by name? He knew that their condition would be miraculously improved if only he could share with them in the power of God's Spirit. It was for that power that he prayed.

In short, our prayers are to be directed toward effectiveness in witnessing: the opportunity to witness (Col. 4:3), the courage to witness (Eph. 6:19), the message of witness (Eph. 6:19). We must focus our prayers on having God's blessing and help as we act in his name.

Second, the Bible instructs us to actively seize opportunities whenever they arise. We are to respond to God-sent chances to reveal God's love rather than allowing them to slip through our fingers, never to be recaptured.

John Greenleaf Whittier spoke the truth when he declared, "For of all sad words of tongue or pen, the saddest are these: 'It might have been!' " To realize that we didn't but might have taken action can make us feel regret, especially when another's eternal destiny is at stake.

In the Book of Romans, Paul offers timely advice for the growing Christian (12:9–13). One of his instructions is: "Seize your opportunities" (v. 11b).[5] Another source

5. The rendering *seize your opportunities* is provided by William Barclay. He offers this background and explanation: "The ancient manuscripts vary between two readings. (Romans 12:11b) Some read, 'Serve the Lord,' and some read 'Serve the time,' that is, 'Grasp your opportunities.'

The ancient scribes used contractions in their writing. The most common words were always abbreviated. A common way of abbreviating was to leave out the vowels, as shorthand does, and to place a stroke along the top of the remaining letters. The word for 'Lord' is *Kurios*, and the term for 'time' is *kairos*. The abbreviation for both of these is *krs*. In th[is] section [that is] so offers the alternative rendering: "Meet the demands of the hour." In other words, the past cannot be recalled. We have only the present in which to reveal God's love to others. Concentrate on spontaneous acts of kindness, willing acceptance of his responsibilities, and especially an ever-ready witness that is adaptable and from the heart. As Peter so aptly put it, we must "always be prepared to give an answer to everyone who asks [us] to give the reason for the hope that [we] have. Do this with gentleness and respect . . ." (1 Peter 3:15b–16a).

Third, after praying for (and receiving guidance in) our action, and being in a perpetual state of readiness to respond to whatever opportunities come our way, we must prepare for the inevitable conflict that will occur. Doing invariably involves conflict, especially doing what is right and helpful.

Biblical metaphors of the Christian life are battle words. Paul portrays us in a contest—a fight, a wrestling match, a race. Hear him as he declares, "For we wrestle not against flesh and blood, but against principalities, against powers, against the rulers of the darkness of this world, against spiritual wickedness in high places" (Eph. 6:12, KJV).

Again, the apostle to the Gentiles triumphantly states, at the close of his life: "I have fought the good fight, I have finished the race, I have kept the faith" (2 Tim. 4:7). For the terms *struggle* and *fight,* Paul employs the Greek words *agōn* and *agōnizomai.* From these ancient terms we get our English words *agony* and *agonize.* Perseverance, suffering, and intense struggle are implied.

Timothy, who had a Greek father, was familiar with the Olympic Games, commonly referred to as *Agōn,* "the noble agony." Therefore, he understood well when Paul exhorted him to "fight (*agōnizomai*) the good fight of the

filled with practical advice, it is more likely that Paul was saying to his people, 'Seize your opportunities as they come.' " William Barclay, *The Daily Study Bible: The Letter to the Romans,* 2d ed. (Philadelphia: Westminster, 1957), pp. 178–79.

faith" (1 Tim. 6:12). In other words, give your best to the one contest of eternal importance.

We must keep one thing in mind. The apostle Paul never employs the term *agōn* in a negative way. Jim McKay on ABC's "Wide World of Sports" often refers to the "thrill of victory and the agony of defeat." But that's Jim McKay, not Paul. The agony that Paul alludes to is the opposite of defeat. Instead, it is the cry of victory: "I have agonized!"[6]

To not agonize and to opt for comfort rather than the conflict that will inevitably occur in the excellent Christian's life is to lose sight of the One we serve. Jesus was the supreme combatant of satanic power. He is described by the writer of Hebrews as the One who "learned obedience from what he suffered" (5:8), the "author and perfecter of our faith, who for the joy set before him endured the cross, scorning its shame" (12:2).

We are invited to "consider him who endured such opposition from sinful men, so that [we] will not grow weary and lose heart" (12:3). In our day it is easy to lose sight of the real Jesus and to picture him as a synthetic, counterfeit Lord who neatly conforms to our hedonistic cravings. But be not deceived. This is not the Christ we serve.[7]

6. Edward Kuhlman, "God's Strugglers in an Age of Video Sainthood," *His*, December 1983, p. 9.

7. Kuhlman offers a dramatic statement concerning our tendency to take the easy way of inaction. As Judy Garland sang in "Somewhere Over the Rainbow," we see the world as a "giant lemon drop." Such a sugar-coated perspective is in sharp contrast to the one our Lord had. In Kuhlman's words: "Is a Christian one who having been found by Christ (the supreme battler of all satanic power) 'wraps the draperies of his couch about him and lies down to pleasant dreams'? Are we guilty of A. W. Tozer's indictment that because Christ did all the dying we think we can romp into heaven? Do we not feel the surge of struggle—the desire to enter the conflict—the true war? . . . .

Struggle? The only struggle some people have is fitting the body into the snug designer jeans commercially cloned from fashion houses. We wear the world's brand on our hip pockets and wonder why we lack identity. Paul the struggler said: 'I bear on my body the marks of the Lord Jesus'. (Galatians 6:17) The Lord's signature was Paul's identity, branded on his body. Elisabeth Elliot has rightly said that we will know who we are when we know whose we are. Designers don't determine identity. God does. And if we agonize, it will become clear when the victory is won." Ibid., p. 10.

Nor does an easy-going attitude characterize the "great cloud of witnesses" (12:1) spoken of by the author of Hebrews. Every one agonized in a fight against evil's powerful forces. But with God's all-wise and all-powerful guidance, they became truly excellent through obedience in action, in loving deeds, and in the midst of severe, unrelenting persecution.

We too must act in spite of the cost. Our witness cannot be tucked away in a warm and safe spot. It must be open, up front, and transparent—which means it will be vulnerable to Satan's weaponry. But with Christ—who endured the ultimate persecution for us—we will prevail. Not somehow. Triumphantly![8]

In no uncertain terms, God's Word commands us to join in the battle for truth. We must prepare our hearts by praying for fighting skills. We must alert our minds to opportunities so that we might respond immediately. We must expect plenty of opposition and struggle. It all adds up to a call to action!

Are there a few suggestions that might assist us as we wage our battle against Satan? What might we keep in mind as we act?

A Ration Pack for Doers

Check lists can be helpful, particularly when you're embarking on a journey. And our Christian life is exactly that, a journey. Some reminders for those of us who are involved in godly, assertive action follow.

There are no plateaus in the Christian life. We must move ahead in action in order to survive.[9] In effect, to not act is to retreat.

8. An inspirational book, *Not Somehow, But Triumphantly!*, was written by the late dean emerita of Eastern Nazarene College, Bertha Munro.
9. The ancient Roman soldier typically wore a breastplate, leather straps to his thigh, sandals, helmet, and shinboards of cork and wood. But there was

Doing must never take the place of being. As excellent Christians, we must excel in both (see the story of Mary and Martha, Luke 10:38–42).

We must lovingly do continuously. To await the big opportunity before acting is to lose valuable, fleeting opportunities to act in small ways.[10]

It is important that we distinguish between loving action and wheel-spinning busy work. The former increases, while the latter saps, spiritual energy.[11]

no protection in back. He would not be tempted to turn around in retreat. As long as we march forward with deeds of loving action, we have spiritual protection.

10. A God-directed act is never to be considered insignificant. It is much like the small finlike vortex blades on a giant aircraft. Although they are small in comparison to other parts of the plane, their function is crucial. They manufacture enough turbulence on a still day for landing. Concerning small things, Ed Young is right in declaring: "Think naughty a trifle, tho it small appear./Small sands make a mountain./Moments make a year, and trifles, life."

11. Virginia Watts Smith, in "How Filling the Time with Good Activity Can Lead to Emptiness," confronts wheel-spinning busyness in the life of the Christian. Not recognizing Christ's lordship is one reason for living such an existence. In addition, she lists these problems: "(1) *Misinterpreting Scripture.* Not really understanding what Jesus meant when he said, 'I must be about my Father's business', nor really knowing how to accomplish the work he wants us to do. (2) *Being insecure.* Thinking we must work hard and fast to get (and keep) the approval of God—and others. (3) *Believing we are indispensable.* 'If I don't do it, nothing will get done'. (4) *Somehow feeling infallible.* 'Oh, I couldn't do anything that wrong', or 'I'm fine. Nothing will happen to me'. (5) *Being guilt-ridden.* 'I feel so guilty if I don't accomplish all the things he/she wants me to do'. (6) *Pride.* 'I'm important. Just look at all the things I accomplish', or 'I can do it better'. (7) *False sense of values.* Temporal, not according to God's eternal values system. (8) *Improper use of time.* 'My time is really not my time. It belongs to God, and I will be accountable to him for use and *misuse* of this valuable commodity'. (9) *Martyr complex.* 'Well, if I die, I'll die working for God'. (10) *Trying to be perfect.* Paul, in Philippians 3:12 said, 'Not that I have already obtained in all this, or have already been made perfect . . .' God has an ideal, certainly and wants us to work toward becoming that person he wants us to be. But God also wants us to be realistic. He knows we're human; after all, he created us. (11) *Not learning to say 'no'.* A definite weakness in many Christians. (12) *Selfish.* 'I want to do *what* I want to do, *when* I want to do it, *how* I want to do it, and no one is going to stop me'. (13) *Not learning to delegate.* Read Exodus 18. (14) *Becoming more concerned about quantity than quality.*" *Eternity,* January 1981, p. 49.

Actions, based on our convictions, must become increasingly independent of the reactions of others. God alone must become our guide.[12]

We must be aware of the numerous, rewarding derivatives of Christian action: self-confidence, lessening anxiety (It's better to do rather than stew), closer fellowship with Jesus and others, motivating others to act, an increasing supply of God's grace.[13]

It must always be remembered that it is never too late

12. William McCumber, in an editorial entitled "Leadership Paradoxes," has listed ten conclusions about people in general. He found the latter in a newspaper article about Howard Ferguson, a wrestling coach, who initially formulated the list. "(1) People are illogical, unreasonable, and self-centered. Love them anyway. (2) If you do good, people will accuse you of selfish, ulterior motives. Do good anyway. (3) If you are successful, you win false friends and true enemies. Succeed anyway. (4) The good you do today will be forgotten tomorrow. Do good anyway. (5) Honesty and frankness make you vulnerable. Be honest and frank anyway. (6) The biggest men with the biggest ideas can be shot down by the smallest men with the smallest ideas. Think big anyway. (7) People favor underdogs, but follow only top dogs. Fight for a few underdogs anyway. (8) What you spend years building may be destroyed overnight. Build anyway. (9) People really need help, but may attack you if you do help them. Help them anyway. (10) Give the world the best you have and you'll get kicked in the teeth. Give the world the best you have anyway."

McCumber adds, "The news article called these Howard Ferguson's 'Paradoxical Commandments of Leadership.' They form . . . an interesting commentary upon our Lord's words: 'It is more blessed to give than to receive.' The value of an action lies, not in the response it will receive, but in the quality of the action itself. Doing what is right, because it is right and honors God, is abundantly worthwhile, whether or not it is understood, appreciated, or reciprocated." *Herald of Holiness,* 15 September 1982, p. 17.

13. Daring to act does entail risk, but offers the potential for great dividends. For example, it has been found that it is more politically expedient to run for an office and lose than to have not run at all. By running you have attained some visiblity.

A few years ago I made a list of ten risk-containing actions that I would pursue. I reasoned the chances were that I would be successful in five of them—which would not have occurred if I had done nothing. As for the five "failures," they only produce learning experiences for future trials. With a few midcourse corrections, they can eventuate in successes. In addition, there is the potential for "spin-offs" in relationship to the five successes. They can multiply, opening up other areas of opportunity and eventual success. All of this adds up to one conclusion: It is foolish to not try. There is too much potential for success.

for us to perform loving actions. Although opportunities might have been missed in the past, there are always other ones in the present.

The Time of Her Life

It is often difficult to see the far-reaching significance of our loving acts. We tend to be so caught up in the present.

Several years ago there were three junior-high-school girl friends who walked home from school together. As they walked, they usually discussed such things as the latest records, boyfriends, and clothing styles.

Two of the girls were sisters, one of whom was later to become my wife. In contrast to the other girl, Emily, the sisters were Christians. And as Christians, they continuously sought opportunities to lead their friend to Christ.

It was summer, and time for Christian youth camp at Santa Cruz. Emily was invited to go and she accepted. The other teen-agers were sure to like her. She had beautiful red hair and the ability to say interesting things when she talked. In the junior high school she was popular and was known as "the brain."

Without Emily's knowledge, a gentleman in the church donated a large portion of her camp fee. It was the only way she could afford to go. In addition, the camp staff positions were filled by adults who lovingly volunteered their services. They sacrificed their time, knowing what a difference a Christian camp experience can mean in the lives of young people. And it did for Emily.

She became totally immersed in the various activities offered: athletic contests, crafts, and perhaps even a "customary" prank or two. But it was the time of her life for a more important reason. One evening, at the close of a soul-stirring message, her two friends noticed that the Holy Spirit's conviction had captured Emily's heart. They proceeded to discreetly invite her to give her life to Jesus.

Her response was immediate. The three girls made their way to the altar to pray.

In a brief time, Emily looked up with a wide smile. The load of sin had been lifted. She had become a born-again Christian. The presence of God reigned supreme in her life. Everything would be different when she returned home.

The time to return came all too soon. Suitcases were packed and good-bys were said. All the way home there was singing and recounting memories. Then it was home at last. The girls separated. The sisters went to their home and Emily went to hers. But they departed as Christians.

Involved in catching up with their summer chores, the sisters didn't have an opportunity to see their friend for a week or two. Then one day they took a notion to stop by her house. Emily was in bed, and Emily's mother sadly informed them that she should not be disturbed.

Soon thereafter school started. But there was no Emily. Again the two sisters walked the four blocks to Emily's house. They were met by her grim-faced mother who invited them in. Then she spoke shocking words: "Girls, your friend Emily is going to die. She has a brain tumor."

Intense grief seized the girls. Not their friend Emily! It couldn't be. They were so close. They had shared so many wonderful times together. Surely she would get better. But she didn't. In a matter of days Emily died.

Her death, although tragic, did have a bright spot: she died a Christian. She would live with Jesus for eternity. Someday they would see their friend in heaven again. That fact was the only one that brought comfort to the hearts of the sisters.

God was able to transform Emily's life because his followers decided to act. Such actions made it possible for her to attend camp and experience life-changing fulfillment. One man provided the money. A pastor constantly encouraged the youth to attend. Volunteers sacrificially and effectively ran the camp program. And, yes, there were the two sisters. They refused to give up until their good friend had met their Best Friend face to face. A long chain of loving actions. A soul born into eternity!

Was it worth all the effort? Let's remember that question. Someday, in the not-too-distant future, we can ask Emily.

A Parting Word

If we are to escape hearing the siren call to excellence, we will be forced to withdraw from the America of the 1980s, for our land is filled with the ringing sound.

Advertisers promise excellence. Politicians pretend to have it. Educators promote it. Athletes perform excellently.

Commercial slogans about excellence abound from sea to shining sea.

We're the mark of excellence. (General Motors)

Putting our energy into excellence. (Atlantic Richfield)

We deliver excellence 95,000 times a day. (Express Mail)

Seminars, conventions, and conferences focus on the theme. Our president has established the Commission on Excellence in Education. Bearing the motto *Commitment to Excellence,* the Los Angeles Raiders won the Super Bowl.

But with excellence receiving such top billing, what

185

ever happened to success? Is it removed from our con-
sciousness and completely forgotten?

Far from it! Motivation to succeed is as strong as ever.
It's just that today excellence is seen as the means of its
attainment. If excellence is the onstage performance, success is the director who calls the shots behind the curtain.

Some declare this is to be an interim condition, and I
hope they are right. May the day come when excellence
is valued for itself. It is a standard that yields far-reaching,
long-lasting, intrinsic reward. The ancient Greeks discovered this fact and thrived.

But what does the issue of success versus excellence
have to do with those of us who attempt to serve Jesus?
Success, even as an interim goal, is a completely unscrip-
tural motivation for our lives. Power, prestige, privilege,
and wealth must not be showcased in our minds and affections. When we possess them, they must be played
down, generously shared, and continuously rededicated to
the Master. Even a cursory reading of the Sermon on the
Mount provides strong support for this position.

In contrast, biblical excellence *is* our mission. It is a
legitimate standard with which to provide wise guidance
for our lives. It is worthy of our utmost attention and
deepest commitment.

Why is biblical excellence so valuable? It includes all
the Christian virtues, but places the spotlight on *agape*
love, the unconditional, God-breathed love that separates
those of us who have welcomed his kingdom into our
hearts from those who serve Satan. Therefore, biblical excellence is not optional. It is essential. We accept it at the
offset of our walk with God, and grow in it as we journey
along the Christian way.

As such growth occurs, we will notice ourselves developing a Christ-like spirit. As the late Bill Draper stated,
we become increasingly

>slow to suspect—quick to trust;
>slow to condemn—quick to justify;
>slow to offend—quick to defend;
>slow to expose—quick to shield;
>slow to belittle—quick to forbear;
>slow to provoke—quick to conciliate;
>slow to resent—quick to forgive.

We drift away from mediocrity. Our lives take on fulfillment and meaning, joy and peace. Our perspective becomes his perspective; our reward, his reward.

May we all hold high, and clutch tightly, the banner of Christian excellence. Today. Tomorrow. For eternity.

Thus a world that is attracted to secular excellence will increasingly come to embrace our kind of excellence, the excellence of authentic, divine love. It is placed in our hearts as a gift of God.

>From the conscience that shrinks from new truth.
>From the laziness that is content with half-truths.
>From the arrogance that thinks it knows all truth.
>Oh, God of truth, deliver us.
>
>—Ancient Hebrew prayer

Trenton Spiritual Gifts Analysis

Introduction

Every Christian has received from the Holy Spirit a certain gift or gifts. As Paul states in Romans 12:6, "God has given each of us the ability to do certain things well." In this way, the Holy Spirit displays God's power through each of us as a means of building the entire church. It then becomes our Christian duty to put these gifts into action for the benefit of the Kingdom.

Before taking this analysis, you should understand four fundamental prerequisites for spiritual gift discovery. To definitely identify your spiritual gift(s) you must:

1. *Be a Christian.* You must be a committed member of the Body of Christ.
2. *Believe in Spiritual Gifts.* You must accept the fact that God has blessed you with one or more gifts.

189

3. *Be Willing to Work.* You must intend to do the job
   for which your spiritual gift(s) has equipped you. God
   will not show you your gift(s) just to satisfy your
   curiosity.
4. *Pray.* You must pray before, during, and after this
   process. Since God wants you to discover your gift(s),
   He certainly will guide and direct you as you attempt
   to identify them.

As you begin the process of discovering your spiritual
gift(s), keep in mind that the results will show you how
you are equipped to serve the Lord, helping to build up
the church, the Body of Christ, to a position of strength
and maturity...to the point of being filled full with Christ.

The Trenton Spiritual Gifts Analysis is an exercise to
help give you a handle on what your spiritual gift(s) might
be. It is adapted from a questionnaire that was originally
designed by Richard F. Houts (*Eternity*, May 1976, pp. 18–
21) and later revised by C. Peter Wagner of Fuller Evangelistic Association. The Trenton version was first developed and used at Saint Paul Lutheran Church in Trenton,
Michigan.

[To gain the full value of this exercise, you should use
it in conjunction with more extensive teaching about spiritual gifts and/or under the guidance of your pastor or
group leader. Additional copies of this questionnaire may
be ordered from the Fuller Evangelistic Association, Box
989, Pasadena, California 91102.]

1. Go through the list of eighty-five statements on the
   Trenton Spiritual Gifts Analysis. For each one, say
   to yourself, "This statement has been experienced in
   my life..." and then check the appropriate box:
   "Much," "Some," "Little," or "Not at All."
2. When you are finished, follow the directions [on page
   200] for scoring the questionnaire.
3. Next, looking at the "Total" column of the Trenton

Gifts Chart on page [200], enter below in the "Dominant" section the three gifts on which you received the highest scores. Then enter in the "Subordinate" section the next three highest-scoring gifts. This will give you a *tentative* evaluation of where your gifts may lie.

Dominant:

1. _____
2. _____
3. _____

Subordinate:

1. _____
2. _____
3. _____

Trenton Spiritual Gifts Analysis*

This statement has been satisfactorily experienced in my life:	Much (3)	Some (2)	Little (1)	Not at All (0)
1. Easily delegating important responsibilities to other people.	☐	☐	☐	☐
2. Finding pleasure in the drawing and/or designing of various objects.	☐	☐	☐	☐
3. Knowing that the repair and maintenance of things in my environment comes easily to me.	☐	☐	☐	☐
4. Leading other people to a decision for salvation through faith in Christ.	☐	☐	☐	☐

This statement has been satisfactorily experienced in my life:	Much (3)	Some (2)	Little (1)	Not at All (0)
5. Speaking words of encouragement to those who are troubled, discouraged, or not sure of themselves.	☐	☐	☐	☐
6. Managing money well in order that I can give liberally to the work of the Lord.	☐	☐	☐	☐
7. Assisting key leaders to relieve them, so they can get back to their main job.	☐	☐	☐	☐
8. Providing food and/or lodging graciously and willingly to people who are in need.	☐	☐	☐	☐
9. Praying for other people and often losing track of the time.	☐	☐	☐	☐
10. Having the ability to discover new truths for myself.	☐	☐	☐	☐
11. Persuading other people to accomplish preset goals and objectives.	☐	☐	☐	☐
12. Working joyfully with and helping those people who are ignored by the majority of others around them.	☐	☐	☐	☐
13. Joyfully singing praises to God either alone or with other people.	☐	☐	☐	☐
14. Being able to effectively play a musical instrument.	☐	☐	☐	☐
15. Enjoying the fact that I am called on to do special jobs.	☐	☐	☐	☐
16. Being able to help other people learn Biblical facts and details which aid in the building up of their lives.	☐	☐	☐	☐

This statement has been satisfactorily experienced in my life:	Much (3)	Some (2)	Little (1)	Not at All (0)
17. Being able to formulate my thoughts and ideas into effective written forms.	☐	☐	☐	☐
18. Having the ability to organize ideas, things, time, and people for more effective results.	☐	☐	☐	☐
19. Finding joy in painting pictures or in other craft objects.	☐	☐	☐	☐
20. Working with various items manually and receiving enjoyment from it.	☐	☐	☐	☐
21. Sharing joyfully with other people how Jesus has brought me to Himself.	☐	☐	☐	☐
22. Enjoying the working out of complicated problems in other people's lives.	☐	☐	☐	☐
23. Giving my money liberally to the work of the Lord.	☐	☐	☐	☐
24. Helping in small ways that oftentimes seem to be behind the scenes.	☐	☐	☐	☐
25. Enjoying having guests in my home.	☐	☐	☐	☐
26. Finding myself praying when I should be doing other things.	☐	☐	☐	☐
27. Knowing that the insights I possess and share with other people will bring changes in attitude and conviction to my fellow Christians.	☐	☐	☐	☐

This statement has been satisfactorily experienced in my life:	Much (3)	Some (2)	Little (1)	Not at All (0)
28. Being able to lead other people toward the accomplishment of specified tasks.	☐	☐	☐	☐
29. Talking cheerfully with the elderly, the shut-in person, or those in jails or prisons.	☐	☐	☐	☐
30. Leading others in singing songs of praise to God or for pure enjoyment.	☐	☐	☐	☐
31. Being involved in a church, school, or local instrumental music presentation.	☐	☐	☐	☐
32. Enjoying routine work at church that would seemingly bore other people.	☐	☐	☐	☐
33. Enjoying the times I share my knowledge, the knowledge of others, and/or the love of Christ with children and/or adults.	☐	☐	☐	☐
34. Feeling secure in the fact that the words I write will be of benefit to those who read them.	☐	☐	☐	☐
35. Being able to work with facts and figures with positive results and personal satisfaction.	☐	☐	☐	☐
36. Finding joy in lawn care and other outside maintenance.	☐	☐	☐	☐
37. Enjoying the pleasures of the out-of-doors, gardening, landscaping, and other projects.	☐	☐	☐	☐
38. Enjoying meeting other people and sharing with them the joy and peace which Jesus and His love have given me.	☐	☐	☐	☐

This statement has been satisfactorily experienced in my life:	Much (3)	Some (2)	Little (1)	Not at All (0)
39. Being able to apply truth to my life effectively on a day-to-day basis, no matter what kind of crisis or conflict may arise.	☐	☐	☐	☐
40. Feeling that I should give much to the Lord for all that He has done and is doing for me.	☐	☐	☐	☐
41. Typing, filing, or recording figures or minutes for the Lord's work.	☐	☐	☐	☐
42. Having guests and/or visitors in my presence and making them feel welcome and a part of things.	☐	☐	☐	☐
43. Feeling secure in the fact that my prayers continually work miracles in my life and in the lives of other people.	☐	☐	☐	☐
44. Acquiring and mastering new facts and principles which can be applied to given situations to aid others in their growth and stability.	☐	☐	☐	☐
45. Knowing that others follow me and the examples I set because I have knowledge which contributes to the building of my church.	☐	☐	☐	☐
46. Visiting in hospitals and/or retirement homes and knowing that my presence has helped in comforting and cheering those people with whom I have come in contact.	☐	☐	☐	☐

This statement has been satisfactorily experienced in my life:	Much (3)	Some (2)	Little (1)	Not at All (0)
47. Singing familiar Gospel songs alone or with groups of fellow Christians.	☐	☐	☐	☐
48. Utilizing my instrumental music talents for the appreciation of my friends and to the glory of God.	☐	☐	☐	☐
49. Feeling satisfaction in doing menial tasks for the glory of God.	☐	☐	☐	☐
50. Teaching children and/or adults about the love of Jesus and feeling that their faith is strengthened through my leadership.	☐	☐	☐	☐
51. Composing and/or arranging newspaper or newsletter articles in an efficient, meaningful style.	☐	☐	☐	☐
52. Planning and administering programs which will be of benefit to my fellow Christians.	☐	☐	☐	☐
53. Enjoying the times that I am able to create beautiful items, especially when they benefit others.	☐	☐	☐	☐
54. Finding that I enjoy maintaining and repairing things in my environment which others have not been good stewards of.	☐	☐	☐	☐
55. Seeking out unbelievers in a continual manner in order to win them for Jesus.	☐	☐	☐	☐
56. Being able to effectively counsel those people who are perplexed or confused, guilty or addicted.	☐	☐	☐	☐

This statement has been satisfactorily experienced in my life:	Much (3)	Some (2)	Little (1)	Not at All (0)
57. Feeling deeply moved when I am confronted with urgent financial needs in the work of God's Kingdom.	☐	☐	☐	☐
58. Distributing tracts, Gospel literature, or other papers in my neighborhood and surrounding community.	☐	☐	☐	☐
59. Willing to open my home to guests and/or strangers and share with them what I have.	☐	☐	☐	☐
60. Feeling that when I am asked to pray for others my prayers will have tangible results.	☐	☐	☐	☐
61. Reading and studying a great deal in order to build myself up in the understanding of Biblical truths.	☐	☐	☐	☐
62. Being able to lead small or large groups of people in decision-making processes.	☐	☐	☐	☐
63. Helping other people with the knowledge that those whom I have helped will do little, if anything, in response to my action.	☐	☐	☐	☐
64. Finding much joy and pleasure in the seemingly simple routine of singing hymns and other Gospel selections.	☐	☐	☐	☐
65. Knowing that my ability to perform instrumental music has helped others grow has given me much satisfaction.	☐	☐	☐	☐

This statement has been satisfactorily experienced in my life:	Much (3)	Some (2)	Little (1)	Not at All (0)
66. Willing to take orders rather than give them.	☐	☐	☐	☐
67. Presenting and discussing Biblical stories with other people and feeling that those people will be edified through me and the power of the Word of God.	☐	☐	☐	☐
68. Finding much pleasure in composing and writing paragraphs and stories for the edification of others.	☐	☐	☐	☐
69. Being able to set goals and objectives and to make plans to reach and accomplish them.	☐	☐	☐	☐
70. Finding that when I work with my hands at various arts and crafts, I derive much joy and satisfaction.	☐	☐	☐	☐
71. Knowing that the knowledge I have when it comes to building or repairing objects is of benefit to others gives me satisfaction.	☐	☐	☐	☐
72. Speaking to other people a message which is primarily the Gospel of salvation.	☐	☐	☐	☐
73. Choosing from several Biblical alternatives an option which usually aids in comforting or directing other people.	☐	☐	☐	☐
74. Willing to maintain a lower standard of living in order to benefit God's work.	☐	☐	☐	☐
75. Finding joy in being an aide to someone who can utilize my help and concern.	☐	☐	☐	☐

This statement has been satisfactorily experienced in my life:	Much (3)	Some (2)	Little (1)	Not at All (0)
76. Having the ability to make strangers, visitors, and guests feel at home when they are with me.	☐	☐	☐	☐
77. Praying is one of my favorite spiritual exercises.	☐	☐	☐	☐
78. Knowing that I am able to distinguish key and important Biblical truths and facts is beneficial to me and others as members of the Body of Christ.	☐	☐	☐	☐
79. Being able to motivate other people in a satisfactory, positive manner.	☐	☐	☐	☐
80. Comforting a fellow Christian during sickness or times of problems and/or anxiety.	☐	☐	☐	☐
81. Singing is one of my favorite spiritual exercises.	☐	☐	☐	☐
82. Finding pleasure in playing a musical instrument, either alone or with other... people.	☐	☐	☐	☐
83. Enjoying it when others express a need for my help.	☐	☐	☐	☐
84. Sharing my knowledge of the love of Christ with children and/or adults in an effective and meaningful manner.	☐	☐	☐	☐
85. Knowing that my literary skill will aid other people and that they will be built up and informed because of it.	☐	☐	☐	☐

Trenton Gifts Chart

In the grid below, enter the numerical value of each of your responses next to the number of corresponding statement on pages 191–99.

Much = 3   Some = 2   Little = 1   Not at All = 0

Now add up the five numbers that you have recorded in each row, placing the sum in the "Total" column.

Rows	Value of Answers					Total	Gift
A	1 2	18 1	35 3	52 0	69 0	6	Administration
B	2 0	19 2	36 0	53 1	70 3	6	Craftsmanship (artistic)
C	3 0	20 1	37 0	54 0	71 1	2	Craftsmanship (manual)
D	4 1	21 3	38 2	55 0	72 0	6	Evangelism
E	5 1	22 1	39 2	56 0	73 0	3	Exhortation-Wisdom
F	6 3	23 3	40 3	57 3	74 2	14	Giving
G	7 1	24 3	41 2	58 2	75 3	11	Helps
H	8 3	25 3	42 3	59 3	76 3	15	Hospitality
I	9 2	26 1	43 2	60 1	77 2	8	Intercession
J	10 1	27 1	44 0	61 1	78 1	4	Knowledge
K	11 0	28 1	45 1	62 0	79 0	2	Leadership
L	12 2	29 1	46 1	63 2	80 2	8	Mercy
M	13 1	30 0	47 0	64 1	81 1	3	Music (vocal)
N	14 0	31 0	48 0	65 0	82 0	0	Music (instrumental)
O	15 3	32 2	49 2	66 3	83 3	13	Serving
P	16 1	33 2	50 1	67 1	84	6	Teaching
Q	17 0	34 0	51 0	68 0	85 0	0	Writing

Review of Gift Definitions and Scripture References

The following . . . pages contain *suggested* definitions of the spiritual gifts covered by this analysis. . . . While not meant to be dogmatic, these definitions and their supporting Scriptures do correspond to characteristics of the gifts as expressed in the Trenton Spiritual Gifts Analysis.

A. Administration

The gift of administration is the special ability to understand clearly the immediate and long-range goals of a particular unit of the Body of Christ, and to devise and execute effective plans for the accomplishment of those goals.

Scriptural references: Prov. 24:3–4; Acts 6:1–7; 15:7–12; Rom. 12:8; 1 Cor. 12:5, 28; 1 Tim. 5:17

B, C. Craftsmanship

The gift of craftsmanship is the special ability to use your hands, thoughts, and mind to further the Kingdom of God through artistic, creative means. People with this gift may also serve as leaders for others in forming their abilities in this area. The gift may also be used in the areas of maintenance, care, and upkeep for the benefit and beautification of God's Kingdom here on Earth.

Scriptural references: Exod. 30:22–25; 31:3–11; 2 Chron. 34:9–13; Acts 8:3; 16:14

D. Evangelism

The gift of evangelism is the special ability to share the Gospel with unbelievers in such a way that men and women become disciples of Jesus and responsible members of the Body of Christ.

Scriptural references: Acts 5:42; 8:5–6; 10:36; 11:20; 13:32; 21:8; Rom. 10:15; Eph. 4:11; 2 Tim. 4:5

E. Exhortation-Wisdom

The gift of exhortation-wisdom is the special ability to minister words of comfort, consolation, encouragement, and counsel to other members of the Body in such a way that they feel helped and uplifted. A person with this gift has insight and understanding of life situations which arise, perceiving what to do and how to do it.

Scriptural references: Acts 6:3–10; 14:22; Rom. 12:8; 1 Cor. 2:1–13; 12:8; 2 Cor. 9:2; 1 Tim. 4:13; Heb. 10:25; 2 Peter 3:15

F. Giving

The gift of giving is the special ability to contribute material resources to the work of the Lord with great joy, eagerness, and liberality.

Scriptural references: Mal. 3:10; Mark 12:41–44; Luke 18:12; Rom. 12:8; 2 Cor. 9:1–7; 9:2

G. Helps

The gift of helps is the special ability to invest one's talents in the life and ministry of other members of the Body, thus enabling the persons helped to increase their effectiveness in the use of their gifts.

Scriptural references: Mark 2:3–4; Acts 9:36; Rom. 16:1–2; 1 Cor. 12:18; 1 Tim. 6:2; 1 Peter 4:9–10

H. Hospitality

The gift of hospitality is the special ability to provide an open house and warm welcome for those in need of food and lodging, to care for those not in the immediate family with joy and effectiveness.

Scriptural references: Acts 16:15; 21:16–17; Rom. 12:9–13; 16:23; Heb. 13:1–2; 3 John 5–8

I. Intercession

The gift of intercession is the special ability to pray for extended periods of time on a regular basis, and also to see frequent and specific answers to one's prayers to a degree much greater than a fellow Christian who does not have an intercessory gift.

Scriptural references: Acts 12:1–17; 16:25–31; Col. 4:12; 1 Tim. 2:1–8; James 5:14–16

J. Knowledge

The gift of knowledge is the special ability to discover, accumulate, analyze, and clarify information and ideas that are pertinent to the growth and well-being of the Body.

Scriptural references: Rom. 15:14; 1 Cor. 12:8; 13:8

K. Leadership

The gift of leadership is the special ability to set goals in accordance with God's purpose for the future and to communicate these goals to others in such a way that they voluntarily and harmoniously work together to accomplish these goals for the glory of God.

Scriptural references: Acts 6:2–4; 7:10; 15:7–12; Rom. 12:8; Heb. 13:17

L. Mercy

The gift of mercy is the special ability to feel genuine concern and compassion for individuals, both Christian and non-Christian, who suffer distressing physical, mental, or emotional problems, and to translate that compassion into cheerfully done deeds that reflect Christ's love and alleviate their suffering.

Scriptural references: Luke 10:33–35; Acts 9:36; 16:33–34; Rom. 12:8; 1 Thess. 5:14

M, N. Music

The gift of music is the special ability to use one's voice in the singing of praises and joy to the Lord for the benefit of others or to play a musical instrument to the praise of the Lord and for the benefit of others.

Scriptural references: Deut. 31:22; 1 Sam. 16:16; 1 Chron. 16:41–42; 2 Chron. 5:12–13; 34:12

O. Serving

The gift of serving is the special ability to identify the unmet needs involved in a task related to God's work and to make use of available resources to meet those needs and help accomplish the desired goals.

Scriptural references: Luke 22:22–27; Rom. 12:7; 2 Cor. 8:19–29; 2 Tim. 1:16–18

P. Teaching

The gift of teaching is the special ability to communicate information relevant to the health and ministry of the Body and its members (children and/or adults) in such a way that they will learn and be edified.

Scriptural references: Acts 18:24–28; 20:20–21; Rom. 12:7; 1 Cor. 12:28; Eph. 4:11; 1 Tim. 3:2

Q. Writing

The gift of writing is the special ability to formulate thoughts and ideas into meaningful written forms so that the reader will find courage, guidance, knowledge, or edification through the words shared with him.

Scriptural references: Ps. 45:1; Acts 15:19–20; Phil. 3:1; 1 Tim. 3:14–15; Jude 3

Discovery of Your Spiritual Gifts

You have now just begun a process of discovering your spiritual gifts. As you reflect on the gifts you have tentatively identified through the Trenton Spiritual Gifts Analysis, try to discern which ones truly are or are not your gifts. To do so, follow this five-step approach.

Explore the possibilities. Read through the three key chapters in holy Scripture dealing with spiritual gifts (1 Cor. 12, Rom. 12, Eph. 4). Learn what the gifts are, what characterizes them, and how they function in the Body of Christ, so that you can have something concrete to look for as you move ahead.

Experiment with as many gifts as possible. The spiritual gifts analysis which you have just completed has helped you experiment with different gifts. Your feelings, reactions, and general outlook on the gifts were measured as you worked through the statements. . . . Now you need to experiment further with the gifts you pinpointed in the analysis, i.e., the "dominant" and "subordinate" gifts listed on page [191]. Unless you try the gifts this analysis has revealed, you will have a hard time knowing whether you really have them or not. Get involved in a ministry activity that will let you try out these gifts.

Examine your feelings. Since *God* has put the Body together, you will feel fulfilled when [you are] functioning in the proper area. Thus, if you enjoy your attempts to use a particular gift, that is a good sign that you possess that gift. If, however, you dislike the service activities associated with a certain gift, that is a fairly good sign that you do *not* have that gift.

Take time to examine your feelings regarding the gifts you identified through this questionnaire, both in the dominant and subordinate clusters. Are you comfortable with them? Do you feel that they are true reflections of yourself? Do you feel secure in the fact that you will be able to put your gifts to work in the Lord's Kingdom? Pray for the Holy Spirit's help and discernment as you examine your feelings concerning these gifts.

Evaluate your effectiveness. Since spiritual gifts are designed to benefit others, you should see positive results as you use your gift(s). If you do not see results when you experiment with a particular gift, you probably do not have that gift. But it could be that you do not give the gift a fair try, or that it will simply take time for you to learn to use the gift effectively. As you evaluate, pray for the courage to be honest with yourself and with your Lord.

Expect confirmation from the body. No gift can be discovered, developed, and used all on your own. Gifts are given to build up other members of the Body. If you have a gift, other Christians will recognize it and give you con-firmation of it. If you feel that you have a particular gift but no one else agrees with you, then you should take a closer look at yourself and re-evaluate.

And remember, in all these five steps, the key is prayer. The Lord will lead you to accurate discoveries of your gift(s) if you allow Him to guide and direct you in all your endeavors.

Appendix B

Temperament Test

The Greek philosopher and physician Hippocrates (400 B.C.), identified four basic temperament types: sanguine, choleric, melancholic, and phlegmatic. Twentieth-century psychologist Karl Jung formulated four similar types: extrovert feeling type (sanguine); extrovert thinking type (choleric); introvert thinking type (melancholic); and introvert feeling type (phlegmatic).

Recently the four types have been popularized by Tim F. LaHaye.[1] Florence Littauer, after reading LaHaye's books, lectured on the four temperaments throughout North America.[2]

The following descriptions are not precise, nor do all of the characteristics apply to everyone in every case. We are

---

1. Tim F. LaHaye, *Spirit-Controlled Temperament* (Wheaton: Tyndale House, 1966), *Understanding the Male Temperament: What Every Man Would Like to Tell His Wife about Himself...But Won't* (Old Tappan, N.J.: Revell, 1977), and *Transformed Temperaments* (Wheaton: Tyndale House, 1971).

2. Florence Littauer, *Personality Plus* (Old Tappan, N.J.: Revell, 1982).

each a unique blend of the traits. Nevertheless, most of us tend to have one temperament or another.

Sanguines are optimistic, verbose storytellers. They're the "live wires" at parties—emotional, enthusiastic, animated, bubbling with cheer. Such persons make friends easily and love people. They are spontaneous, do not hold grudges, and thrive on compliments.

On the negative side, sanguines crave popularity and being the center of attention. If there is credit to be given, they want it. Often such individuals dominate conversations, fail to listen to others, and interrupt. Sanguines frequently exaggerate, dwell on trivia, and seldom remember names. Their loud voices and laughter can alienate those to whom they appear phony or egotistical. Finally, they are quick to get angry and often seem childish.

Cholerics, like sanguines, are extroverts and optimistic. However, their primary goal is to get things done. They are action people, strong-willed, decisive, confident. Hence, they are leaders—getting things (and people) organized, making changes, and righting wrongs.

They're often perceived as being bossy, impatient, quick-tempered, and under stress. They are competitive and poor losers. They love controversy, are inflexible and unsympathetic, and offer few compliments.

Melancholics are deep, thoughtful people. Many are talented, creative, and gifted in music or art. Others love detail work: graphs, charts, figures—the components of research analysis. Melancholics are sensitive to others, self-sacrificing, and conscientious.

Negatively, such individuals tend to see the dark side of life. They can easily become moody and depressed because they focus too much on themselves and their feelings.

Phlegmatics are introverts and pessimists who would rather observe than participate. They have few enemies because they're casual, relaxed, cool. In addition, they are well-balanced, consistent, and quiet. Although they keep their emotions hidden, phlegmatics are mostly sympathetic and kind.

On the other hand, phlegmatics can be so low-key they appear unenthusiastic and boring. At times their laid-back exterior masks worries and fears. Often they are indecisive, making them the last to volunteer for responsibilities. Although they seem easy-going, at times they are hiding a stubborn, selfish steak.

To summarize, think of the four types in these ways:

Sanguines: Happy, chatty, forgetful.

Cholerics: Leaders, drivers, dominating.

Melancholics: Thinkers, perfectionists, sensitive.

Phlegmatics: Calm, easy-going, indecisive.[3]

The Temperament Test

This word-association test was developed by Florence and Fred Littauer and has been used with thousands of participants in their "Personality Plus" seminars. In each of the following rows of four words across, place an X in front of the *one word* that *most often applies* to you. Be sure to mark one word on each line, even if, in some cases, the choices do not fit you exactly. From each set of four words, pick the one that *comes closest* to describing you. For instructions on how to score the test, see page 211.

1 __ Animated	__ Adventurous	__ Analytical	__ Adaptable
2 __ Persistent	__ Playful	__ Persuasive	__ Peaceful
3 __ Submissive	__ Self-sacrificing	__ Sociable	__ Strong-willed
4 __ Considerate	__ Controlled	__ Competitive	__ Convincing
5 __ Refreshing	__ Respectful	__ Reserved	__ Resourceful
6 __ Satisfied	__ Sensitive	__ Self-reliant	__ Spirited

3. Based on information from Fritz Ridenour, *What Teenagers Wish Their Parents Knew About Kids* (Waco: Word, 1982).

7 __ Planner	__ Patient	__ Positive	__ Promoter
8 __ Sure	__ Spontaneous	__ Scheduled	__ Shy
9 __ Orderly	__ Obliging	__ Outspoken	__ Optimistic
10 __ Friendly	__ Faithful	__ Funny	__ Forceful
11 __ Daring	__ Delightful	__ Diplomatic	__ Detailed
12 __ Cheerful	__ Consistent	__ Cultured	__ Confident
13 __ Idealistic	__ Independent	__ Inoffensive	__ Inspiring
14 __ Demonstrative	__ Decisive	__ Dry humor	__ Deep
15 __ Mediator	__ Musical	__ Mover	__ Mixes easily
16 __ Thoughtful	__ Tenacious	__ Talker	__ Tolerant
17 __ Listener	__ Loyal	__ Leader	__ Lively
18 __ Contented	__ Chief	__ Chartmaker	__ Cute
19 __ Perfectionist	__ Permissive	__ Productive	__ Popular
20 __ Bouncy	__ Bold	__ Behaved	__ Balanced
21 __ Brassy	__ Bossy	__ Bashful	__ Blank
22 __ Undisciplined	__ Unsympathetic	__ Unenthu-siastic	__ Unforgiving
23 __ Reluctant	__ Resentful	__ Resistant	__ Repetitious
24 __ Fussy	__ Fearful	__ Forgetful	__ Frank
25 __ Impatient	__ Insecure	__ Indecisive	__ Interrupts
26 __ Unpopular	__ Uninvolved	__ Unpredictable	__ Unaffectionate
27 __ Headstrong	__ Haphazard	__ Hard to please	__ Hesitant
28 __ Plain	__ Pessimistic	__ Proud	__ Permissive
29 __ Angered easily	__ Aimless	__ Argumentative	__ Alienated
30 __ Naive	__ Negative attitude	__ Nervy	__ Nonchalant
31 __ Worrier	__ Withdrawn	__ Workaholic	__ Wants credit
32 __ Too sensitive	__ Tactless	__ Timid	__ Talkative
33 __ Doubtful	__ Disorganized	__ Domineering	__ Depressed
34 __ Inconsistent	__ Introvert	__ Intolerant	__ Indifferent
35 __ Messy	__ Moody	__ Mumbles	__ Manipulative

36 — Slow	— Stubborn	— Show-off	— Skeptical
37 — Loner	— Lord over others	— Lazy	— Loud
38 — Sluggish	— Suspicious	— Short-tempered	— Scatter-brained
39 — Revengeful	— Restless	— Reluctant	— Rash
40 — Compromising	— Critical	— Crafty	— Changeable

Scoring Instructions

To score the Temperament Test, transfer your marks on pages 209–11 to this sheet, add up your strengths and weaknesses, and combine both sets of totals to see which temperaments are the strongest.

Strengths			
Sanguine	*Choleric*	*Melancholic*	*Phlegmatic*
1 — Animated	— Adventurous	— Analytical	— Adaptable
2 — Playful	— Persuasive	— Persistent	— Peaceful
3 — Sociable	— Strong-willed	— Self-sacrificing	— Submissive
4 — Convincing	— Competitive	— Considerate	— Controlled
5 — Refreshing	— Resourceful	— Respectful	— Reserved
6 — Spirited	— Self-reliant	— Sensitive	— Satisfied
7 — Promoter	— Positive	— Planner	— Patient
8 — Spontaneous	— Sure	— Scheduled	— Shy
9 — Optimistic	— Outspoken	— Orderly	— Obliging
10 — Funny	— Forceful	— Faithful	— Friendly
11 — Delightful	— Daring	— Detailed	— Diplomatic
12 — Cheerful	— Confident	— Cultured	— Consistent
13 — Inspiring	— Independent	— Idealistic	— Inoffensive
14 — Demonstrative	— Decisive	— Deep	— Dry humor

15 __ Mixes easily	__ Mover	__ Musical	__ Mediator
16 __ Talker	__ Tenacious	__ Thoughtful	__ Tolerant
17 __ Lively	__ Leader	__ Loyal	__ Listener
18 __ Cute	__ Chief	__ Chartmaker	__ Contented
19 __ Popular	__ Productive	__ Perfectionist	__ Permissive
20 __ Bouncy	__ Bold	__ Behaved	__ Balanced
Totals _____	_____	_____	_____

Weaknesses

Sanguine	Choleric	Melancholic	Phlegmatic
21 __ Brassy	__ Bossy	__ Bashful	__ Blank
22 __ Undisciplined	__ Unsympathetic	__ Unforgiving	__ Unenthusiastic
23 __ Repetitious	__ Resistant	__ Resentful	__ Reluctant
24 __ Forgetful	__ Frank	__ Fussy	__ Fearful
25 __ Interrupts	__ Impatient	__ Insecure	__ Indecisive
26 __ Unpredictable	__ Unaffectionate	__ Unpopular	__ Uninvolved
27 __ Haphazard	__ Headstrong	__ Hard to please	__ Hesitant
28 __ Permissive	__ Proud	__ Pessimistic	__ Plain
29 __ Angered easily	__ Argumentative	__ Alienated	__ Aimless
30 __ Naive	__ Nervy	__ Negative attitude	__ Nonchalant
31 __ Wants credit	__ Workaholic	__ Withdrawn	__ Worrier
32 __ Talkative	__ Tactless	__ Too sensitive	__ Timid
33 __ Disorganized	__ Domineering	__ Depressed	__ Doubtful
34 __ Inconsistent	__ Intolerant	__ Introvert	__ Indifferent
35 __ Messy	__ Manipulative	__ Moody	__ Mumbles
36 __ Show-off	__ Stubborn	__ Skeptical	__ Slow
37 __ Loud	__ Lord over others	__ Loner	__ Lazy
38 __ Scatter-brained	__ Short-tempered	__ Suspicious	__ Sluggish

39 — Restless   — Rash   — Revengeful   — Reluctant

40 — Changeable   — Crafty   — Critical   — Compromising

    Totals _____   _____   _____   _____

    Combined
    Totals _____   _____   _____   _____

Subject Index

Acceptance, need for, 124–26
Accessibility, 85–87
Actions. *See* Loving actions
Acts of Paul and Thecla, 94
Adam, 58, 126–27
Administration, gift of, 201
Adversity, 176–78; glorifying God in, 67, 68; overcoming, 24–25
Affluence. *See* Wealth and possessions
Agapē (love), 48–50, 140; entire sanctification and, 59; as excellence, 69; growth in, 73. *See also* Excellence, biblical; Love, authentic
Agōn (struggle), 176, 177
Agonize, positive sense of, 176–78
Agōnizomai (to fight), 176
Alexander the Great, 46
Aretē (excellence): biblical meaning of, 47–49, 51; definition of, 49n; Greek ideal of, 38–41, 50
Aristotle, 37, 50n
Armerding, Hudson: on Christian excellence, 48
Assertive actions. *See* Loving actions

Assimilation, 126. *See also* Fellowship
As You Like It (Shakespeare), 107
Attainability of excellence, 50
Augustine, 141
Availability, 85–87
Awareness of others, 87–88

Barclay, William, 167; on seizing opportunities, 175–76n; on servanthood, 78n, 79
Barth, Karl, 91
Beatitudes, 94
Belonging, need for, 124–26
Bernstein, Leonard: on sacrificing, 81
Bigotry-brotherhood paradox, 132
Bridges, Jerry: on glorifying God, 66
Brown, John Mason: on goals, 29
Bultmann, Rudolf: on Hellenism, 50n
Burnout, 156–57
Busy-work, 179
Bystander effect, 173

Calkin, Ruth Harms, 89

Campolo, Anthony, Jr., 16, 29; on
    success fantasy, 31
Channing, William Ellery, 104
Chase, J. Richard, 45
Cheap grace, 12
Choleric personality type,
    characteristics of, 208
Cicero, 35
Clergy, as motivators, 160. *See also*
    Minister; Ministry
Coggins, Wade: on evangelization,
    71
Colson, Charles: on success gospel,
    64
Compassion, 167–68
Competition, 78; as counterfeit
    motivation, 64
Compromise, 142–43
Confession of sins, 56–57
Conflict resolution, 131
Conformity, 56, 138, 147
Consecration, 57–59
Constancy, 59–60
Conviction(s), 137–50; assertive
    actions and, basis of, 180; as
    barriers to change, 140–41;
    biblical perspective on, 144–46,
    148; biblical principles versus,
    148; compromise of, 142–43;
    consistent, 140, 145; discernment
    of, 143, 148; false, 139–41;
    liberating power of, 141, 145–46;
    need for, 137–39; negative, 141;
    selfish, 140; steadfastness in, 146–
    50; suffering for, 149–50;
    superstitions versus, 139–40;
    witnessing through, 149. *See also*
    Obedience
Conviction rut, 141
Courage, 59, 168–69
Craftsmanship, gift of, 201
Creation, 126–27
Cromwell, Oliver: on pursuit of
    excellence, 25
Cronyism, 130
Culbertson, Paul T.: on need for
    excellence, 70

Darley, John M., 173n
Darrach, Brad: on status, 31–32
Deceitfulness, 82–83. *See also* Role
    playing
Deeds of excellence, 53–56. *See also*
    Loving actions
Dependency on God, 94–96. *See
    also* Openness
Desperation, 100
Diomede, 37
Discernment, 67, 143, 148
Discipline, 53–54
Discouragement, 123
Dishonesty, 114. *See also* Role
    playing
Doubt, 100
Doulos (servant), 78
Draper, Bill, 186–87
Dunne, John: on social nature of
    persons, 125

Earle, Ralph: on love and Christian
    excellence, 49n
Ekecheiria (cessation of hostilities),
    36
Elitism, 129
Elliot, Elisabeth, 177n
Emerson, Walt, 137
Empathy, 168
Entire sanctification. *See*
    Sanctification, entire
Erwin, Gayle D.: on disciples, 95–96
Euripides, 137
Evangelicalism, growth of, 12
Evangelism, gift of, 201
Evangelization, 59, 71. *See also*
    Witnessing
Excellence: characteristics of, 25;
    examples of, 24–25; Japanese and,
    27n; need for, 24; pursuit of, 25–
    26; ripple effect of, 26;
    satisfaction intrinsic to, 26;
    universal call to, 26; voluntary
    nature of, 26–27. *See also*
    Excellence, biblical; Excellence,
    secular

Excellence, biblical, 45–60; as *agapē*
(love), 48–50, 69; boomerang
effect of, 71; call to, 12; centrality
of, 186; deeds of, 53–56;
definitions of, 48–49; as divine
attribute, 51 n. 6, 54; glory of God
and, 51–52; growth in, 71–73;
misconceptions about, 15–16; as
mission, 186; need for, 70; as
openness to God, 56–61;
preparation for, 54–55; ripple
effect of, 70, 71; source of, 51–52;
in thought, 52–53; universal
availability of, 50; use of *aretē* to
define, 45–48
Excellence, secular, 35–41;
characteristics of, 33; cost of, 34;
as end in itself, 39; goals of, 78,
93; Greek ideal of, 35–41; human
effort as source of, 52; as means
to success, 186; motivating power
of, 39–40; need for, 34; perfection
as, 38, 39; preeminence as, 38;
promotion of, 185–86; restricted
availability of, 50; success versus,
29–34; superiority as, 38; virtue
as, 38. *See also* Success, secular
Exhortation-wisdom, gift of, 201–2

Faith, 47 n; confession of sins and,
56–57; Jesus as author and
perfecter of, 68
Fanaticism, 140
Fatalism, 173
Fellowship, 121–35; basis of, 127;
biblical perspective on, 126–28;
commitment to building, 130–33;
as goal of mission, 127–28;
human need for, 124–26;
incorporation/assimilation of
newcomers into, 132–35; lack of,
125; effects of, 125; obstacles to, 128–
30; positive effects of, 126
Fletcher, Joseph, 138 n
Frost, Robert, 151

Gandhi, Mahatma, 91

Gardner, John W., 21; on pursuit of
excellence, 25
Garlow, James L.: on laity as
ministers, 159
Generosity, 163; of Jesus, 78;
servanthood and, 78, 82
Genuineness, 117. *See also*
Honesty; Simplicity
Gifts. *See* Spiritual gifts
Giving, gift of, 202
Glorification of God, 66–73; in
adversity, 67, 68; excellence as,
51–52, 67; investment of self as,
67–68; Jesus as model for, 68–69;
as motivating goal, 64; results of,
69–71; spiritual gifts and, 163–
65; spiritual growth through, 71–
73; transformation of world by,
69–71
Glover, T. R., 45
God, counterfeit images of, 64. *See
also* Glorification of God; Love of
God
Goethe, Johann Wolfgang von: on
Greek ideals, 40
Gortner, Marjoe, 110
Gospel of success, dangers of, 64–66
Grace: cheap, 12; confession of sins,
56–57; entire sanctification, 57–
59
Gratitude: openness to presence of
God and, 99; simplicity and, 102–
3
Greek communities, early church
ministry to, 46–47
Greek ideals, 35–41; biblical
authors and, 47–48, 50n; Jesus
and, 45–46
Grider, J. Kenneth, 45; on *agapē*, 49;
on conversion of Saul, 122n; on
entire sanctification, 58n; on self-
disclosure, 118
Groupie-bums, 117
Guilt, 56, 127

Hagiazō (to sanctify), 59
Hallucinations, 112

Hellenism. *See* Greek ideals
Helps, gift of, 202
Hesiod, 37
Hippocrates: on temperament, 172, 207
Hod (glory), 51
Holiness, excellence as, 12, 14
Holiness movement, 57 n. 9, 58 n
Holy Spirit, 181; confession of sins and, 57; as guide to truth, 148; indwelling of, 99–100; reliance on, 96; self-disclosure and, 118
Homer, 37
Honesty: Christian identity and, 119; of Jesus, 115–17; role playing and, 109, 112–14. *See also* Genuineness; Simplicity
Hope, 55, 68
Hospitality, gift of, 202
Houts, Richard F., 190
Humboldt, Alexander von: on Greek ideals, 40
Huxley, T. H., 54
Hypocrisy: biblical condemnation of, 114–15; legitimate, 107–8

Impatience, 56
Incorporation/Assimilation Scale, 134
Ineptitude, 21–24
Inferiority, feeling of, 153–54
In Search of Excellence (Peters and Waterman), 12, 15, 27 n
Intercession, gift of, 202–3
"I Wonder" (Calkin), 89

Japanese, pursuit of excellence by, 27 n
Jefferson, Charles Edward: on sincerity of Jesus, 115, 116 n
Jesus Christ: approval of, 62; as combatant of satanic power, 68–69; as embodiment of divine love, 68–69; false images of, 68, 177; generosity of, 78; as hope, 68; influence of Hellenism on, 45–46; as *Kurios*, 79; as living example, 69; ministry of, to Greeks, 46;

obedience of, 68, 177; on possessions/wealth, 98; prayer of, 174–75; reconciling death of, 69; on servanthood as standard of excellence, 79–81; servanthood of, 82; sincerity and honesty of, 115–17, 149; social status of, 97–98; struggle of, against satanic power, 177; on thoughts and attitudes, 52–53
John XXIII (pope), 91
Johnston, Leo Charles, Sr., 121
Jones, E. Stanley: on hope, 68
Joy, 162
Judgment of others, 148–49
Jung, Karl: on temperament, 207

Kairos (time), 175 n
Kelley, Dean M., 141 n
King, Martin Luther, Jr.: on overcoming adversity, 24–25
Kinghorn, Kenneth, 160
Knowledge: gift of, 203; insufficiency of, 62–63
Koinōnia (fellowship), 128
Kuhlman, Edward: on false images of Jesus, 68
Kurios (Lord), 79, 122 n, 175 n

LaHaye, Tim F., 207
Laos (layman), 159
La Rochefoucald, François de, 105
Latane, Bibb, 173 n
Layman, as minister, 159–60
Leadership, gift of, 203. *See also* Servanthood
Lee, Earl G., 61, 99 n; on rest in God, 63 n
Legalism, 63
Leon, Harry J., 46 n. 1
Lewis, Carl: on Christian success, 162–63
Lifestyle, Christian, 12–13
Lincoln, Abraham, 151
Lindbergh, Charles, 77
Linkage, 126. *See also* Fellowship
Linkletter, Art, 137
Littauer, Florence, 207, 209

Littauer, Fred, 209
Livingstone, R. W., 35; on *aretē*, 38, 39; on perfection, 39
Logos (word), biblical meaning of, 47n
Love, authentic, 49–50, 69; constancy and growth of, 59–60; counterfeit motivations for, 63–66; as ground of discipline, 55; necessity of, for salvation, 60; as sign of service, 55; supremacy of, 49
Love of God: openness to, 110; as source of divine action in history, 174
Love webs. *See* Fellowship
Loving actions, 167–83; avoidance of, reasons for, 171–73; biblical perspective on, 169–71, 174–78; checklist of reminders for, 178–81; deeds defeating, 56; excellence in, 53–56; as expression of thanksgiving, 100–101; importance and value of, 181–83; persevering/agonizing in, 176–78, 180; praying for, 174–75; readiness for, 175–76; rewarding derivatives of, 180; "seizing opportunities" for, 175–76, 179, 180–81
Lowell, James Russell: on pursuit of excellence, 34
Lynch, James J.: on value of being sociable, 126

McCheyne, Robert Murray, 55; on Jesus as embodiment of divine love, 68
McCumber, William: on assertive actions, 180 n. 12
McGinnis, Alan Loy, 121
Maintenance activities, versus authentic mission, 128–29
Marasmus, 124–26
Marty, Martin: on bigotry-brotherhood paradox, 132; on Christian excellence, 48
Mask wearing. *See* Role playing

Materialism, 98. *See also* Wealth and possessions
Mathews, Shailer, 77
Maturity, Christian, 59–60, 72
Mediocrity, 56; as institutional characteristic, 11; replacement of, 187
Meekness, 96
Melancholic personality type, characteristics of, 208
Mercy, gift of, 203
Merit, 63
Minister, layman as, 159–60. *See also* Clergy
Ministry, as exercise of spiritual gifts, 159–61
Mission: biblical excellence as, 186; fellowship as goal of, 127–28; maintenance activities versus, 128–29
Mitchell, Curtis: on witness prayer of Jesus, 174
Money. *See* Wealth and possessions
Moody, Jess: on convictions, 145–46
Moors, Mark: on love and Christian excellence, 49
Motivation, 61–73; counterfeit, 63–66; glorification of God, 66–69; need for, 63; pursuit of excellence as, 39–40; for success, 32
Multiple personalities, 112
Munro, Bertha, 178 n. 8
Murphy's Law, 23–24
Murray, Andrew, 61
Music, gift of, 203
"My Symphony" (Channing), 104

Nee, Watchman: on worldly success, 147
Nepotism, 129–30
Nonexcellence, 21–24

Oath-taking, 116
Obedience: biblical command of, 144; bite-the-bullet, 63; consistent, 138; of Jesus, 68, 177. *See also* Conviction(s)

Ogilvie, Lloyd: on human need for socialization, 125
Oikonomia (household), 159
Olympic athletes (ancient), motivation of, 35–37
Openness, 56–61, 110, 114, 178
Optimism, 173
Original sin, 58
Owens, Jesse, 55

Parents, effect of, on role playing, 110–11
Parker, Cecil, 61
Partners in Ministry (Garlow), 159
Passing the buck, 172–73
Patterson, Virginia: on need for excellence, 70
Peace, 88–89
Perfection: as goal of Christian life, 11; Greek ideal of, 38, 39. See also Excellence, biblical
Pericles, 35
Perseverance, 178
Peters, Thomas J., 12, 15, 27n
Petition, prayer of, 99, 100
Philostratus the Elder, 53
Phlegmatic personality type, characteristics of, 208–9
Pistis (faith), biblical meaning of, 47n
Pius XI (pope), 45
"Plain Account of Christian Perfection" (Wesley), 140–41
Plato, 35, 37
Possessions. See Wealth and possessions
Power, 186; definition of, 30; servanthood and, 12; success as, 30. See also Success, secular
Powerlessness, 13. See also Servanthood
Prayer: for effective witnessing, 174–75; simplicity and, 98–103
Prayer of petition, 99, 100
Prayer of thanksgiving, 98–101
Preeminence, 38
Prestige, 186; abandonment of, 12. See also Success, secular

Priorities, false sense of, 128–29
Privilege, 186; definition of, 30; success as, 30
Progressive excellence, 71
Projection, 149
Purkiser, W. T.: on love and Christian excellence, 49n

Rebellious persons, social unacceptability of, 108
Rejection, 122–23
Rest, spiritual, 63n
Richards, Larry: on Christian excellence, 48
Ridenour, Fritz: on false standards, 139; on hesitancy to act, 171; on worldliness, 145
Ripple effect, 26, 70, 71
Risk taking, 172, 180
Ritualism, negative, 141
Robinson, Haddon: on Christian excellence, 48
Rockefeller, John D.: on stewardship, 158
Role playing, 105–19; avoidance of pain through, 111; characteristics of appropriate, 109–10; misrepresentation of facts through, 112–14; negative reasons for, 110–14; parental influence on, 110–11; status and, 111–12
Rosch, Paul, 29

Sacrifice, 13; as demand of servanthood, 81–82
Sanctification, entire, 57–59; instantaneousness of, 57–58; results of, 58–59
Sanguine personality type, characteristics of, 208
Satan, 63, 68, 88, 147–48
Schaible, Cynthia R.: on gospel of success, 65
Schedules, as barriers to servanthood, 85–87
Self: distortions of, 112; "I" versus "me," 108, 109

Self-assertion, 168. *See also* Loving actions
Self-concept, 117; negative, sources of, 53
Self-discipline, 53–54
Self-disclosure, 117–19
Self-esteem, 111–12, 117
Self-identity, 117
Self-investment, 67–68
Selfishness, 140
Self-righteousness, 116
Sensitivity to others, 87–88
Sermon on the Mount, 88
Servant, 78–79. *See also* Servanthood
Servanthood, 13, 77–89; accessibility/availability for, 85–87; awareness of others and, 87–88; biblical ideal of, 78–81; deceitfulness in living, 82–83; deeds of, 55–56; fundamentals of mastering, 85–89; glorification of God by, 88–89; growth in, meaning of, 79; inappropriate attempts at, 83–84; obstacles to, 81–85; power and, 12; privacy of, 89; rejection of, by others, 88; sacrificing for, 81–82
Servant of Christ, 79
Serving, gift of, 204
Shakespeare, William: on role-playing, 107
Shame, 127
Shaw, George Bernard, 105
Shelley, Percy Bysshe: on Greek ideals, 40
Shyness, 153–54
Simplicity, 91–104; biblical perspective on, 93–101; carbon copy, 101; dependency on God versus ability and, 94–96; external, 103–4; gratitude and thanksgiving and, attitude of, 98–101; internal, 102–3; of lifestyle, 12; need for, 92–93; sacrifice versus affluence and, 96–98; suggestions for practicing, 102–4. *See also* Genuineness; Honesty

Sin, confession of, 56–57. *See also* Satan; Temptations
Sincerity, 114–17; effects of, on self-esteem, 117–19; Jesus as model of, 115–17
Situation ethics, 138n
Snyder, Howard, 132 n. 8
Social conformity, 56, 138, 147
Social disengagement, 125
Socialization, human need for, 124–26. *See also* Fellowship
Social webbing, 126. *See also* Fellowship
Specialization, 157
Sphere of influence, 158–59
Spinoza, Baruch, 21; on social nature of persons, 125
Spiritual gifts: analysis of, 161, 189–206; biblical list of, 160; discovery, process for, 204–6; purpose of, 189–90; uniqueness of, 158–59
Spiritual gifts, specific, 160; administration, 201; craftsmanship, 201; evangelism, 201; exhortation-wisdom, 201–2; giving, 202; helps, 202; hospitality, 202; intercession, 202–3; knowledge, 203; leadership, 203; mercy, 203; music, 203; serving, 204; teaching, 204; writing, 204
Spiritual gifts, use of, 151–65; being approved of God through, 161–62; biblical perspective on, 157–63; burnout in, 156–57; dependence on God for, 161; failure in, 153–54; generosity in, 163; glorifying God by, 163–65; as ministry, 159–61; procrastination in, 154–57; resistance to, 152–53; responsibility for, 158–59, 163–64, 189; roadblocks to, 153–57; specialization in, 157
Spiritual growth, gift of, 71–72
Spiritual refurbishing, 72
Spiritual renovation, 72
Standards. *See* Conviction(s)

Stapert, John: on glorifying God, 67
Status: achievement of, through role
    playing, 111–12; success as, 30–
    32
Stereotype-prejudice-discrimination
    syndrome, 39 n. 7
Stewardship, 163–65. See also
    Spiritual gifts, use of
Stricture, versus stringency, 141 n
Struggle, of Christian, 176–78. See
    also Adversity
Success, Christian, rewards of, 162–
    63
Success, secular, 12–13, 29–34, 147;
    characteristics of, 33; as
    compromise of biblical values, 16;
    as counterfeit motivation, 64;
    definition of, 30; excellence
    versus, 29–34; motivation for, 32;
    power as, 30; privilege as, 30;
    reward of, 162; status as, 30–32;
    wealth as, 30
Success Fantasy (Campolo), 16
Success fantasy, 31–32
Success gospel, dangers of, 64–66
Success theology, 12–13
Sullivan, Bill M., 121
Superiority, 38
Superstitions, 139–40
Swindoll, Charles R.: on Christian
    fellowship, 131
Systemics, 126. See also Fellowship

Talents. See Spiritual gifts
Taylor, Kenneth: on need for
    excellence, 70
Teaching, gift of, 204
Temperament, types of, 171–72,
    207–9; choleric, 208; melancholic,
    208; phlegmatic, 208–9; sanguine,
    208
Temperament test, 209–13
Temptations, 56; compromise, 143;
    discouragement, 123; worldliness,
    144–45
Thankfulness. See Gratitude
Thanksgiving, prayers of, 98–101
Thomas, D. Paul, 97

Thomas, W. Ian: on Jesus as living
    example, 69
Thoughts: excellence in, 52–53;
    importance of, 53
Timidity, 153–54
Tozer, A. W., 177 n. 7
Transparency, 114, 178
Trenton Spiritual Gifts Analysis,
    161, 189–206
Trials. See Adversity
Trueblood, Elton: on conviction, 138
Trust, betrayal of, 56
Truth, discernment of, 148
Truthfulness. See Honesty
Twain, Mark, 91

Unblocked interfacing, 114
Unmasking, biblical, 117–19

Vine, W. E.: on aretē, 49 n
Virtue, 38; agapē as, 49–50; aretē
    as, 49; excellence as summary of,
    186–87

Wagner, C. Peter, 190
Waterman, Robert H., Jr., 12, 15,
    27 n
Weakness, as openness to God, 95.
    See also Dependency on God;
    Servanthood
Wealth and possessions: definition
    of, 30; Jesus' view of, 98; sharing
    of, with others, 12; simplicity and,
    96–98; status symbol of, 30;
    success of, 30; world distribution
    of, 98 n. 8
Welch, Reuben: on human need to
    belong, 125
Wesley, John, 29; on fanaticism,
    140; on possessions, 96–97
"Where He Leads," 51
White, Howard A.: on need for
    excellence, 70
White, John: on glorification of God,
    64
Whitehead, Alfred North: on pursuit
    of excellence, 25
Whittier, John Greenleaf, 175

Wilson, John, 46 n. 1, 50n
Wisdom, 47, 59
Witnessing: conflict involved with, 176–78; empowerment for, 59–60; prayer of Jesus for, 174–75
Word (*logos*), biblical adaptation of, 47 n

World, transformation of, 69–71
Worldliness, 144–45, 147
"Worldly squeeze," 142 n
Writing, gift of, 204

Zeus, 35–36, 37 n

Scripture Index

Genesis

2:18—126
3:8–17—114

Exodus

3:11—95
4:1—95
4:10—95
30:22–25—201
31:3–11—201

Numbers

13–14—169
14:10—169

Deuteronomy

31:22—203
34:5—78

Joshua

7:18–26—114
14:7–12—170
14:13—170
24:29—79

Judges

6:15—95

1 Samuel

9:21—95
15:7–22—114
15:22—114
16:7—83
16:16—203
18:18—95
18:23—95
24:14—95

1 Kings

3:7—95

1 Chronicles

16:41–42—203

2 Chronicles

5:12–13—203
34:9–13—201
34:12—203

Job

27:4b—114

Psalms

8:1—51
19:7—93
36:7—73
37:4—99
37:7—63n, 161
34:7b—162
45:1—204
78:70—79
90:10—155
103:12—118
116:6—93
122:1—127

Proverbs

16:25—138
24:3–4—201

Isaiah

20:3—79
53:9—115

224

Ezekiel

17:24—96

Daniel

3—146

Amos

1:8—58
2:1–4—59
3:7—79
4:31—59
7:14—95
15:8–9—58, 59
15:9—58n
26:18—58n

Habakkuk

3:3—51

Zechariah

4:6—96
6:13—51

Malachi

3:10—202

Matthew

3:11—58n
5:3–10—94
5:3–11—50
5:15—153
5:25—131
5:37—116
5:44—174n
6:1–6—88
6:8—65
6:24—98, 148
6:32—65
7:1—149
7:2—149
7:11—100
9:37–38—174
10:24–25—81
10:42—55

11:28–30—117
15:19—52
18:20—127
24:45–51—159, 163
25:18—153
25:21—62
26:6–12—98
26:33—84
26:75—84

Mark

2:3–4—202
10:15—158
10:35–45—64
10:42–44—80
12:41–44—202
12:42–43—98

Luke

7:34—97
7:36—97
10:33–35—203
10:38–42—179
11:13—100
12:15—98
12:16–21—98, 156
12:22–23—65
18:12—202
21:1–4—163
22:22–27—204
22:27—80
23:25—81

John

1:1–5—74n
2:1–2—98
3:16—55
6:7—158
6:9—158
6:35—115
8:12—115
8:44—116
10:7—115
10:10—145
10:11—115
10:14—115

12:3—146
12:25—69
13:4—81
14:2–3—66
14:6—116
14:16–17—73
15:5—47n
15:10—144
15:19—144
16:13—148
17:14—147
17:16–19—59
17:17—58n
19:39—97

Acts

5:42—201
6:1–7—201
6:2–4—203
6:3–10—202
7:10—203
8:3—201
8:5–6—201
9:3–6—122n
9:5—122n
9:10—123n
9:15—122n
9:17—123n
9:22—123
9:26—123
9:27—123
9:36—202, 203
10:36—201
11:20—201
12:1–7—203
13:32—201
14:22—202
15:7–12—201, 203
15:19–20—204
16:14—201
16:15—202
16:25–31—203
16:33–34—203
17:11—148
17:30—56
18:24–28—204
20:20–21—204

21:8—201
21:16-17—202
22:8—122n
28:15b—161

Romans

1:1—79
8:15—99
8:16-17—57
10:1—174
10:9-10—56
10:15—201
12—204
12:1-2—58
12:2—144
12:6—189
12:6-8—160
12:7—204
12:8—93, 201, 202, 203
12:9-13—175, 202
12:11b—175
12:15—131
12:16—131
12:17b—114
13:13—114
15:14—203
16:1-2—202
16:23—202

1 Corinthians

1:9—127
1:17—94
1:27-29—94
2:1-13—202
2:2—65
4:1—78n
7:22b—79
7:23—79
9:22-23—133
9:27—54
10:31—64
12—204
12:4-11—16
12:5—201
12:8—202, 203

12:18—202
12:28—160, 201, 204
12:31—17, 67
13:1-3—66
13:3—140
13:8—203
13:13—49
13:31—49

2 Corinthians

1:12—93
1:22—58n
2:14a—145
2:14b-15—145
2:15—70
3:3—70
3:18—71
5:17—56, 132
7:10—56
8:19-20—204
8:21—114
9:1-7—202
9:2—202
9:7—98, 158
10:10—94
11:3—93
11:23b-30—123
11:30—95
12:9—95
12:10—95

Galatians

1:18—123
2:9—124
2:20—65, 69
4:5-7—99
6:17—177n

Ephesians

1:3—147n
1:13—58n
2:2—147
2:8-9—60, 174
2:10—70
4—204
4:11—160, 201, 204

4:15—72
4:22-24—56
4:26-27—131
4:30—58n
6:6b—79
6:7—147
6:10-18—147n
6:12—176
6:19—175
6:19-20a—175

Philippians

1:10—67, 115
2:3—130
2:4—130
2:5—130
2:12—63
3:1—204
3:14—14
4:4—99
4:6—99
4:7—99
4:8—53, 115

Colossians

2:11— 58n
3:9-11—118
4:3—175
4:12—203

1 Thessalonians

1:2—57n
1:3—57n
1:4—57n
1:6—57n
1:7—57n
2:13—57n
3:12—59
5:14—203
5:23—57n

1 Timothy

2:1-8—203
2:2—174n
2:4—174n
3:2—204

3:14–15—204
4:12—160
4:13—202
5:17—201
6:2—202
6:12—177
6:17—145

2 Timothy

1:11—79
1:16–18—204
2:4–5—201
2:15—71, 160, 162
4:7—176

Titus

3:5—60, 174

Hebrews

4:11—63n
4:12—52
4:16—60, 100
5:8—68, 177
10:25—127, 202
11—47n
11:6—63
12:1—54, 178
12:2—47n, 68, 161,
   177
12:3—68, 177
13:1—202

13:1–2—202
13:8—138
13:17—203
13:18—115

James

1:1—79
1:12—55
1:19—55
1:27—144
2:1—55
2:14—54
2:15–18—55
2:17—54
2:18b—54
3:7–8—55
4:1—55
4:4—55, 144
4:14b—154
4:17—54
5:5—55
5:12—55
5:14–16—203
5:19–20—55

1 Peter

1:5—47n
2:4–5—159
2:9—53
2:9–10—159
2:12—67
2:12a—115
3:15b–16a—176

4:9–10—202
4:11—67
4:12–14—65
4:16—67
5:4—16

2 Peter

1:1—79
1:3—51
1:5—54
1:10b–11—54
3:15—202
3:18—72

1 John

1:3—127
1:7—72, 127
2:15—144
3:16b—87
3:17—87
4:7—51

3 John

5–8—202

Jude

1—79
3—204

Revelation

3:15–16—145